For [barcode]

With much respect and Kindest regards

Bri P. Ja...

Democracy in California

Democracy in California

Politics and Government in the Golden State

Brian P. Janiskee
and
Ken Masugi

ROWMAN & LITTLEFIELD PUBLISHERS, INC.
Lanham • Boulder • New York • Oxford

ROWMAN & LITTLEFIELD PUBLISHERS, INC.

Published in the United States of America
by Rowman & Littlefield Publishers, Inc.
A Member of the Rowman & Littlefield Publishing Group
4720 Boston Way, Lanham, Maryland 20706
www.rowmanlittlefield.com

PO Box 317, Oxford, OX2 9RU, United Kingdom

British Library Cataloguing in Publication Information Available

Library of Congress Cataloging-in-Publication Data

Janiskee, Brian P. 1967–
    Democracy in California : politics and government in the Golden State /
Brian P. Janiskee and Ken Masugi.
        p.   cm.
    Includes bibliographical references and index.
    ISBN 0-7425-2251-2 (cloth : alk. paper)—
    ISBN 0-7425-2252-0 (pbk. : alk. paper)
        1. California—Politics and government. 2. Democracy—California.
    I. Masugi, Ken. II. Title.
    JK8716 .J36 2003
    320.9794—dc21   2002005244

Printed in the United States of America

♾ ™ The paper used in this publication meets the minimum requirements of
American National Standard for Information Sciences—Permanence of Paper for
Printed Library Materials, ANSI/NISO Z39.48-1992.

Dedicated to the memory of
Thomas B. Silver

Contents

Preface

To instruct democracy, if possible to reanimate its beliefs, to purify its mores, to regulate its movements, to substitute little by little the science of affairs for its inexperience, and knowledge of its true interests for its blind instincts; to adapt its government to time and place; to modify it according to circumstances and men: such is the first duty imposed on those who direct society in our day.[1]

Were it an independent nation, observers frequently note, California would be the fifth-largest economy in the world.[2] It would also be the world's strangest democracy. The institutions of federalism and the separation of powers, developed by the U.S. Constitution to enable a large representative democracy to exist, do not characterize California democracy. By contrast, California has a weak, fragmented executive, and local governments depend on the state government in Sacramento for major portions of their budgets. There is no "federal analogy" by which California counties can be compared with American states under federalism.

Often noted as well is the ethnic composition of California, which would make it a major Latino nation. (It also has the largest percentage of Asians and Asian Americans of any continental state.) But diversity and prosperity do not alone explain California's government and why Californians govern the way they do. Such an understanding requires an examination of California history, political traditions, and political character. It is the third-largest state, 770 miles long and 250 miles wide at its most distant points. Mountains, deserts, forests, beaches, farmland, and federally owned land (almost half of the total) bound the habitable areas that contain 35 million people, almost 13 percent of the U.S. population. California remains an attraction for settlers—as it was during the Gold Rush and is for those from abroad today. Do its Pacific and Mexican borders mean an opening to exotic cultures, or are they an invitation to disturbing alien ways? Do they signal opportunity or the need for self-defense?[3]

California's geographical separation from the United States, and the unique circumstances of its entry into the Union via the Compromise of 1850, has enabled an independent political character to develop. A major example of this independence is the power, by majority popular vote, to amend the state constitution. These initiative and referendum powers reflect that defining, still-evolving movement within American politics known as Progressivism, which sought to rid politics of corruption by subjecting it to a new, professionalized, and scientific political process. In many regards, from its professional legislature to its centralization of power in Sacramento, from its mood swings on dealing with race and ethnicity to the initiative and referendum, the Golden State has embodied the spirit and reality of Progressivism. Throughout *Democracy in California* we will note the Progressivist character of California political life, but our primary purpose is to explain California's governmental institutions and how their dynamics affect our lives, for better and for worse. How do we make sense of California politics? How does it reflect democracy's blind instincts, its true interests, or its seemingly boundless opportunities?

In this ambitious effort, as our title reflects, we are guided by Alexis de Tocqueville's classic, *Democracy in America*. What might a student of Tocqueville or, more importantly, of American government say on examining California today? We emphasize that our text presupposes no familiarity whatsoever with the classic text by this nineteenth-century French political theorist and statesman (1805–59); our text stands by itself as a succinct guide to California politics, and is intended for the reader who has some basic familiarity with American government and politics.

We begin with elements of Tocqueville's teaching that seem to characterize many Californians (and other Americans): their indifference to politics, their love of novelty, their desire for wealth and status, and their love of freedom balanced with resentment of those they perceive as privileged. From our first chapter on the diversity of California, as Tocqueville might have perceived it, we develop other Tocquevillean themes in subsequent chapters. The two tasks reinforce each other, making possible a more compelling and, frankly, more interesting understanding of California's political life than hitherto available. In the end, the reader will understand and assess the workings of California politics and government and, with encouragement, become one of Tocqueville's engaged citizens.

While the final product is a mutual effort, the general division of labor in the manuscript's development was as follows: Brian Janiskee wrote chapters 3–7, 9, and 10; and Ken Masugi wrote the introduction and chapters 1, 2, and 8.

We thank the University of Chicago Press for permission to quote extensively from its edition of *Democracy in America*, which was edited and translated by Harvey C. Mansfield and Delba Winthrop. We are grateful to the University of California Press for permission to reprint material from Mark Baldassare, *California at the Millennium: The Changing Social and Political Landscape*. We also wish to thank Viking-Penguin for its kind permission to quote from Richard Rodriguez, *Days of Obligation: Arguments with My Mexican Father*, and Simon & Schuster for its kind permission to quote from Victor Davis Hanson, *The Land Was Everything*.

We are grateful for the support we received in the preparation of this book. Daniel C. Palm of Azusa Pacific University, Richard Reeb of Barstow College, and John J. Pitney, Jr., of Claremont McKenna College read the entire manuscript and offered several helpful suggestions. Jeremy Swanson also proofread portions of the manuscript. Ralph Rossum of Claremont McKenna College gave help and encouragement.

We thank our colleagues and friends at California State University, San Bernardino, for their support and encouragement: Mike LeMay, Al Mariam, Ralph Salmi, Mark Clark, Ed Erler, Bill Green, Scot Zentner, and Debbi Fox. We thank Cheryl Adam, Janice Braunstein, Mary Carpenter, Reid Hester, Lynda Hill, Laura Roberts, John Wehmueller, and all those at Rowman & Littlefield who made this project possible. We also thank Steve Wrinn for his support. We thank the staff at the Claremont Institute for their professional support—especially Judy Day, Penny McWhorter, Nancy Padilla, and Mary Schmall. Howard Ahmanson, senior counselor of the Institute's Center for Local Government, inspired us to write this book. We hope our book reflects the rigor and vigor Harry V. Jaffa has displayed in his investigation of equality in the American political tradition. President Brian Kennedy encouraged each step of the process.

Brian Janiskee wishes to thank his wife, Jennifer, and daughters, Alexandra and Katherine. In addition, he wishes to thank Carol Weissert of Michigan State University for inspiring his interest in state politics. Ken Masugi wishes to thank his daughter, Veronica, and her grandmother Mary. The support and understanding of our families during the completion of this manuscript was more than we could have reasonably expected.

Most of all, we are indebted to the late Thomas B. Silver, president of the Claremont Institute, to whom this book is dedicated. His assistance was not merely self-interest properly understood, to use a Tocquevillean concept. Tom suddenly passed away on December 26, 2001. He will be remembered as a friend, colleague, and ardent champion of the principles of the American Founding.

NOTES

1. Alexis de Tocqueville, *Democracy in America*, trans., ed., and with an introduction by Harvey C. Mansfield and Delba Winthrop (Chicago: The University of Chicago Press, 2000), 7.

2. *Silicon Valley/San Jose Business Journal*, 15 June 2001, <sanjose.bizjournals.com/sanjose/stories/2001/06/11/daily58.html> (accessed 12 April 2002). In 2000, California's economy was worth $1.33 trillion, which placed it slightly ahead of France and behind the United Kingdom.

3. Basic information about California can be found on the following websites: <www.netstate.com/states> (accessed 26 December 2001) and <www.my.ca.gov/state/portal/myca_homepage.jsp> (accessed 26 December 2001).

Introduction

> I confess that in America I saw more than America. I sought there an image of democracy itself, of its penchants, its character, its prejudices, its passions; I wanted to become acquainted with it if only to know at least what we ought to hope or fear from it.[1]

Alexis de Tocqueville (1805–1859) wrote one of the most intriguing books ever published about America and our politics. Even after over 160 years, his two-volume *Democracy in America* remains, in the view of generations of readers and leading scholars, "the best book ever written on democracy and the best book written on America."[2]

Tocqueville was a French aristocrat who toured America for a little more than nine months in 1831–32. Not merely a scholar learned in philosophy, history, and literature, he was also a patriot devoted to politics who later served briefly as Minister of Foreign Affairs during the Second French Republic (1848). Originally, Tocqueville wrote to educate his fellow Frenchmen to the ways of democracy, but his book would make its greatest impression on generations of Americans, beginning with its publication and immediate translation. His 700-page work met with great praise immediately upon its publication, and it continues to be issued in new translations and scholarly editions. His brilliance casts light on topics ranging from education to the role of women, from the influence of money on our character to race relations.[3]

After a civil war, industrialization, immigration, world wars, and a civil rights revolution, this claim of enduring wisdom may appear to be exaggerated. But Tocqueville would have a penetrating explanation for all of these great events and how they shaped the essential character of America and its people. His famous predictions (of, for example, the Cold War division of the world between Russia and America) may be taken to signify his understanding of America. He seems to have put his finger on the heart of what it means to be an American. Even beyond his astounding predictions, what makes him such a great teacher is his ability to speak frankly and persuasively about both our faults and our virtues. One can ransack his book for striking sayings, but that reduces its depth to its surface.

Moreover, even when Tocqueville's 160-year-old analyses seem outdated—for example, in changes to race relations and the place of religion in civic affairs—we have nonetheless a comparison with other eras in America, which can be instructive concerning what we have gained and what we have lost over the years. Are we a freer people than we were fifty years ago? Is there more equality, more liberty, more patriotism? The greatness of Tocqueville's book and its enduring vitality over time rest squarely on its ability to counter our faults. Tocqueville remains ever our teacher, even when we fail to pay attention.

So what can Tocqueville teach us? Consider some Californian and American traits that at first don't seem related to politics, but which we believe go a long way in explaining California. Americans reveal an indifference to politics, a love of wealth, a craving for novelty, an unhealthy individualism, and a jealousy about their equality that can overwhelm even their regard for liberty. Thus, Californians are Americans—Tocqueville's Americans.

Consider the much-bemoaned American indifference to politics. In California only 52 percent of all eligible voters bothered to vote in the November 2000 elections, and voting is considered a minimal sign of involvement in politics. But, according to Tocqueville, we were always a people too busy for politics. And Tocqueville also noted how Americans are in fact political, in ways more significant than voting—for example, in being an active member of a PTA or aiding a charity.[4] Thus, in being indifferent to politics in the narrow sense of holding office, we are being very American—but being overly American in this sense can undo us as a nation. Tocqueville recognized that the American is a complex being—and the Californian no less so—and extremes in any direction can lead to change for the worse.

> Private life is so active in democratic times, so agitated, so filled with desires and work, that hardly any energy or leisure remains to each man for political life. . . .
>
> That such penchants are not invincible I shall not deny, since my principal goal in writing this book has been to combat them.[5]

A "private life . . . filled with desires and work." It becomes too easy for the Californian to confuse work—that is, the money it brings—with the purpose of life.

I do not know a country where the love of money holds a larger place in the heart of man and where they profess a more profound scorn for the theory of the permanent equality of goods.[6]

Our desire for wealth goes hand in hand with our desire for novelty. Americans want the latest clothing styles, CDs, cars, fast-food crazes, and computer programs. But how new must the new be? Should our laws change as quickly as the features at the local movie theater?

The American inhabits a land of prodigies, around him everything is constantly moving, and each movement seems to be progress. The idea of the new is therefore intimately bound in his mind to the idea of the better. Nowhere does he perceive any boundary that nature can have set to the efforts of man; in his eyes, what is not is what has not yet been attempted. . . .

The American taken randomly will therefore be a man ardent in his desires, enterprising, adventurous—above all, an innovator. This spirit is in fact found in all his works; he introduces it into his political laws, his religious doctrines, his theories of social economy, his private industry; he brings it with him everywhere, into the depth of the woods as into the heart of the towns.[7]

But this quest for wealth and for innovation—recall the Gold Rush—has consequences for the way one treats one's family, neighbors, friends, and society in general.

In the West one can observe democracy reaching its furthest limit. In those states, improvised in a way by fortune, the inhabitants arrived only yesterday on the soil they occupy. They hardly know one another, and each is ignorant of the past of his closest neighbor. . . . The new states of the West already have inhabitants; society does not yet exist there.[8]

Tocqueville would later describe this condition as individualism, an unhealthy condition he linked to democratic times.[9] Isolated from one another, men and women lose their ability to act together for common purposes such as improvement of the local schools. They thus become more dependent on governmental authority. The Americans of Tocqueville's era were guided by a religious faith that gave men and women the moral framework that led to strong families, law-abiding behavior, a consistent work ethic, charity, and submission to the standards of a transcendent realm.[10] With changes in Christianity and Judaism and the infusion of new religions from around the world, we have become a somewhat different nation, more vulnerable to the tendencies Tocqueville warned us against.

As much as we individualistically strive for wealth to purchase or find what is new, we affirm our equality with others.[11] In fact, we are so proud of our equality that we resent those who claim to be above us.

> There is in fact a manly and legitimate passion for equality that incites men to want all to be strong and esteemed. This passion tends to elevate the small to the rank of the great; but one also encounters a depraved taste for equality in the human heart that brings the weak to want to draw the strong to their level and that reduces men to preferring equality in servitude to inequality in freedom.[12]

Thus Tocqueville posed the question of how we Americans can reconcile our love for equality with our regard for liberty and excellence.

For a book on California politics, so far we have spoken little of California and perhaps even less on politics. But these Tocquevillean insights are essential for understanding our current political condition. After all, the U.S. is a democratic republic that depends, more than any other form of government, on the character of its citizens to be successful.[13] There can be no politics without citizens. What sorts of citizens are indifferent to politics, obsessed by the pursuit of wealth, isolated from each other, insistent on novelty, and attached to one's equality with each other— perhaps more attached to this than to excellence, especially if greater freedom is perceived in another? Tocqueville's principal goal was to fight the penchants or inclinations that turn us away from a life of active citizenship.

Now, all this is not a complete portrayal of the Californian or of the American. We have omitted, for now, what Tocqueville would have noted about the self-sacrifice of Americans in bloody wars and in modest charity; the rich network of associations ranging from the Boy Scouts to civic groups; and, above all, the vital role of religion in shaping the American character. Tocqueville sought to counter the undesirable facets of the American character with the admirable ones. We are today even more American in many regards that Tocqueville noted. California politics has been decisively shaped by these and other attitudes, and we cannot understand democracy in California unless we consider them and their consequences. *Democracy in California* seeks to consider these in order to foster the spirit of citizenship. We do so through understanding how our democratic character, as portrayed by Tocqueville, has shaped the growth of our political institutions and how those institutions function today. Thus, to paraphrase Tocqueville, in California we see more than California.

NOTES

1. Alexis de Tocqueville, *Democracy in America*, trans., ed., and with an introduction by Harvey C. Mansfield and Delba Winthrop (Chicago: The University of Chicago Press, 2000), 13.

2. Harvey C. Mansfield and Delba Winthrop, introduction to *Democracy in America*, by Alexis de Tocqueville, xvii.

3. Tocqueville, *Democracy*. See also other editions: Tocqueville, *Democracy*, ed. J.P. Mayer, trans. David Lawrence (New York: Harper & Row, Perennial Books, 1988); Tocqueville, *Democracy in America*, ed. Phillips Bradley, based upon the Francis Bowen revision of the Henry Reeve translation, 2 vols. (New York: Random House, Vintage Classics, 1990); and Tocqueville, *Democracy in America*, ed. Sanford Kessler, trans. Stephen D. Grant (Indianapolis: Hackett, 2000).

4. See Robert D. Putnam, *Bowling Alone: The Collapse and Revival of American Community* (New York: Simon & Schuster, 2000); and Francis Fukuyama, *The Great Disruption: Human Nature and the Reconstitution of Social Order* (New York: Touchstone Books, 1999).

5. Tocqueville, *Democracy*, 643.

6. Tocqueville, *Democracy*, 50.

7. Tocqueville, *Democracy*, 387–388.

8. Tocqueville, *Democracy*, 50.

9. Tocqueville, *Democracy*, vol. II, part 2, chapters 2–4.

10. For two contemporary works that emphasize the differences and continuity between Tocqueville's America and ours today see Robert Bellah et al., *Habits of the Heart* (Berkeley: University of California, 1985); and Angelo Codevilla, *The Character of Nations: How Politics Makes and Breaks Prosperity, Family, and Civility* (New York: HarperCollins, Basic Books, 1997).

11. Robert J. Samuelson, "Who Cares How Rich Bill Gates Is?" *Washington Post*, May 2, 2001, A21.

12. Tocqueville, *Democracy*, 52.

13. Alexander Hamilton, James Madison, and John Jay, *The Federalist Papers*, ed. Clinton Rossiter with introduction and notes by Charles R. Kesler (New York: Penguin, Mentor Books, 1999), 346.

Chapter One

From Tribes to One Common Citizenry: California's Diversity

Beyond the frontiers of the Union toward Mexico extend vast provinces that still lack inhabitants. The men of the United States will penetrate into these solitudes even before those who have the right to occupy them. They will appropriate the soil, they will establish a society on it, and when the legitimate proprietor finally presents himself, he will find the desert fertilized and foreigners sitting tranquilly on his inheritance. . . .[1]

When one finally penetrates into the new states of the Southwest, where the social body, formed yesterday, still presents nothing but an agglomeration of adventurers or speculators, one is confounded to see into whose hands public power is placed, and one wonders by what force, independent of legislators and of men, the state can grow and society prosper there. . . . There are certain laws whose nature is democratic and which nonetheless succeed in part in correcting these dangerous instincts of democracy.[2]

Tocqueville was writing about what we know today as Louisiana (which achieved statehood in 1812), Mississippi (1817), and Alabama (1819), followed by Arkansas (1836). Western governments attracted an unsavory set of characters—and the early history of California has certainly borne that out. Reform of the early legislatures became the principal work of the later ones, in an attempt to root out or at least suppress "adventurers" and "speculators."

Like other Americans who moved west, Californians too were willing to adopt different ways as they sought wealth, fled debts, and savored a new way of life. Once they arrived in California, diverse ways of producing wealth created contrasting characters among them. For example, in the Central Valley, which spans inland California from Bakersfield to Stockton:

1

As an agrarian culture, our hard work permeated everywhere, encompassed everyone. . . . I used to see very few cobblestone streets, cappuccino bars, or neighborhood theaters in any of our small [San Joaquin] Valley towns. Instead, the Valley's attraction was always and only its bustle of hardworking agrarian peers, and the bounty that grew out of their endless and uncomplaining work. For all our Valley boosterism, let us confess that there is little tradition of great universities, renowned symphonies, impressive museums, or enclaves of artists between Fresno and Bakersfield. Let us, then, live or die with our strength, which is the wonderful soil, the monotonous climate, and the agricultural genius and good sense of our people, a folk like none other on this planet and whose toil created an oasis.[3]

Farmer and historian Victor Davis Hanson bemoans the loss of farms and the character they instill. Los Angeles and southern California represent something else:

Dreams have a way of struggling towards materialization. Los Angeles did not just happen or arise out of existing circumstances, a harbor, a river, a railroad terminus. Los Angeles envisioned itself, then materialized that vision through sheer force of will. Los Angeles sprung from a Platonic conception of itself, the Great Gatsby of American cities.[4]

Finally, the essayist Richard Rodriguez has speculated on San Francisco's meaning:

For most of its brief life, San Francisco has entertained an idea of itself as heaven on earth, whether as Gold Town or City Beautiful or the Haight-Ashbury.
    San Francisco can support both comic and tragic conclusions because the city is geographically *in extremis,* a metaphor for the farthest-flung possibility, a metaphor for the end of the line, Land's end.

But the metaphor may mislead, and to understand California we may need to supply yet other perspectives, not excluding our own, at least as a start:

To speak of San Francisco as land's end is to read the map from one direction only—as Europeans would read it or as the East Coast has always read. In my lifetime San Francisco has become an Asian city. To speak, therefore, of San Francisco as land's end is to betray parochialism. My parents came here from Mexico. They saw San Francisco as the North. The West was not west for them. They did not share the Eastern traveler's sense of running before the past—the darkening time zone, the lowering curtain.[5]

To think of California in this way is to appreciate both the extremism and the moderation of the Golden State, in a word its reflection of the American character itself.

Southern California tended to be settled by southerners, northern California by northerners (as evidenced by the use of the Iowa and New York Constitutions as models for the first California constitution). Great men rose to the challenges posed by Californians' needs, which included that most basic need of water:

> Working in their special medium, imagined public works, the early water engineers of California were artists and prophets of social and moral development. Prophesying the bringing of water to the desert and to the cities on the plain, they saw themselves embarked upon a work of social redemption Biblical in metaphor and suggestion.[6]

California was a tangible product of the imagination. California represents an incredible diversity of ways of life, attracting streams of people from around the country and world. Unlike many states, California is not restricted to a few sources of wealth. Its natural and technological resources include aerospace, agriculture (cotton, fruits, and nuts), oil and natural gas, real estate, Silicon Valley, and entertainment, and all industries are amplified by export to the rest of the United States and the entire world. The *Statesman's Yearbook 2001* declared that "California is the most diversified agricultural economy in the world."[7] World trading partners include the People's Republic of China, Mexico, and Europe. California Overseas Trade and Investment Offices are found in major world cities, including London, Tokyo, Jerusalem, and Johannesburg.

What does all this diversity mean? As Richard Rodriguez puts it, "Diversity admits everything; stands for nothing."[8] But clearly its most contentious contemporary meaning is political and refers to differences based on race, ethnicity, and gender, and how we should take account of these differences.

Out of a geographically and ethnically diverse collection of inhabitants, drawn to California for different reasons, how do we get one state of citizens? Can there be one nation if ethnic groups look upon others as "they" or even as "the Americans"?[9] How does California prepare its people to be American citizens? The challenges to a common citizenship exist not only geographically—witness the frequent calls for the separation of northern and southern California—but ethnically as well.

The United States was unified through both necessary and noble means, that is, by appealing to the common and the high in human nature.[10] First, one must note the effects described by James Madison in *The Federalist* (no. 10, 1787), of a people bound together by a modern economy, which encourages a diversity of means of employment. Class conflict is minimized as people identify themselves with different liveli-hoods, as well as with their locality or region, which can in turn be absorbed within a national economy. Political unity is fostered by, and fosters, this prepolitical unity based on the mutual satisfaction of needs.[11] As Americans have known from George Washington's farewell address, such economic exchange—such as manufactured goods for agricultural ones—produces national unity in its most elementary form.[12] But full political unity required a bloody civil war. As interpreted by Abraham Lincoln, this war was necessary to affirm the fundamental proposition that justifies the nation's institutions and existence: the self-evident truth of human equality.[13] The nobility and the cosmic signifi-cance of this struggle are explicated in Lincoln's Gettysburg Address. Equality means that each and every individual has certain inalienable rights, including the rights to life, liberty, and the pursuit of happiness. Government must proceed via the consent of all, and thus is by nature limited. This is what the founders of America sought to establish nation-wide, and each state was expected to imitate these general principles of republican government.

What makes any political community one body? A political commu-nity is not simply a pact for the mutual exchange of goods and services. For human beings to become common citizens, they must see beyond their families and their tribes (or nationalities). They must see each other as more than trading partners. In traditional families there is a clear hier-archy: Tribes regard each other with suspicion, as if not sharing a com-mon humanity. Among citizens, as Aristotle (384–322 B.C.) indicates, men and women must regard each other as equals. Aristotle struggles with this key political question of citizenship throughout his writing in *Politics*.[14] His conclusion is that citizens must see themselves as members of a single regime, or constitutional order, that serves the common good—in other words, as citizens. Citizens both obey and rule, and they are better citizens and better men and women for doing so. Abraham Lincoln illustrated the psychology of citizenship in a pre–Civil War speech:

> The man of the highest moral cultivation, in spite of all which abstract princi-ples can do, likes him whom he *does* know, much better than him whom he does *not* know. To correct the evils, great and small, which spring from want of sympathy, and from positive enmity, among *strangers,* as nations, or as indi-viduals, is one of the highest functions of civilization.[15]

Thus, Lincoln combined the wisdom of Aristotle with that of the Found-ing Fathers.

How can a California full of strangers, full of people who by occupation and prejudice oppose and may even oppress each other's interests, become a people of a single citizenship? After all, in a globalized economy one might feel a kinship more to the land of one's trading partners or ancestors than to where one actually lives. As Aristotle taught, the unity of a nation rests on its constitution, laws, and citizens. Let us see how Californians sought to create this unity from the diverse elements of the Golden State. In other words, the study of diversity leads to the study of California's constitution and citizenship.

The study of constitutional government in California reveals a development of principles rooted in its last constitutional convention, which was held in 1878–1879. Although California has changed since then, our constitution and major political developments grew from patterns formed by the constitution of 1879. As much as we may hate to admit it, we Californians are who we are—as human beings in our profoundest and most superficial ways, as citizens with our political passions and passivity—on account of our collective past, regardless of when we or our ancestors arrived in the Golden State.

We can study state government as an example of American constitutional principles at work. In the case of California, we can see what happens to a government that lacks the means of securing the rights that the founders gave America in the Declaration of Independence and the Constitution. In sum, California constitutional history shows us, in the growth of Progressivism, a justification for a politics based on the satisfaction of passions, whether for wealth, status, recognition, or power of whatever kind. There has been a gradual substitution of will for reason and mounting tensions between majoritarian impulse and genuine deliberation. As California government increasingly becomes the instrument for gratifying citizens' needs, these dynamics produce the centralized government Tocqueville feared. With the need for government at both the state and national levels, state governments would eventually become instruments of the national one. The development of California government provides wonderful examples of the American character that we sketched in our previous chapter: apolitical, obsessed with wealth, taken with novelty, and jealous of equality with others.

With this in mind, we reconsider the fabled Gold Rush of 1848. One historian calls the Gold Rush "the most significant event in the first half of the nineteenth century. . . . No other series of events produced so much movement among peoples; called into question so many basic values—marriage, family, work, wealth, and leisure."[16] The Argonauts, as prospectors were called (after the classic Greek heroes who sought the

Golden Fleece), could find instant riches similar to winning the lottery or investing cleverly in the stock market today, but the risky endeavor often entailed leaving behind an anxious family, outraged creditors, or scoffing neighbors. Many struck it rich by hitting pay dirt, but for others the ruinous venture did not pan out. Observers as early as Sir James Bryce, in his classic *The American Commonwealth,* (first published 1886, revised through 1912) reflected on the similarity between mining and gambling and their effects on the California character:

> The chief occupation of the first generation of Californians was mining, an industry which is like gambling in its influence on the character, with its sudden alternations of wealth and poverty, its long hours of painful toil relieved by bouts of drinking and merriment, its life in a crowd of men who have come together from the four winds of heaven, and will scatter again as soon as some are enriched and others ruined, or the gold in the gulch is exhausted.[17]

Surely Gold Rush California is this much of Tocqueville's America in a nutshell: the desire for wealth, novelty, and equality (in the sense of achieving wealth).[18]

But with the boom in California's American population, it became an immediate candidate for statehood and even bypassed territorial status. Much to the grumbling of the South, the **Compromise of 1850** admitted California as a free state, along with addressing other controversial national issues. These included prohibition of the slave trade in Washington, D.C.; territorial status for New Mexico and Utah without reference to slavery; and, most controversial of all for northerners, stricter fugitive slave laws. California tipped the balance between free and slave states, making evident the free future of America, and thus led to the secession of the South and to the Civil War.[19] To understand what it means to be a Californian, one must understand the Civil War—a task we can only call attention to, not undertake, here.

Eagerly anticipating statehood, Californians wrote the **California Constitution of 1849,** and patterned it mostly after the Iowa Constitution but also after that of New York. The early Californians believed, as did the founders of this country, in self-government and all the risks it entailed. We hear as well echoes of the early Massachusetts Bill of Rights of 1780 in the preamble and first article of the constitution of 1849:

> We, the people of the State of California, grateful to Almighty God for our freedom, in order to secure and perpetuate its blessings, do establish this Constitution. . . . All men are by nature free and independent, and have certain inalienable rights, among which are those of enjoying and defending life and

liberty; acquiring, possessing, and protecting property; and pursing and obtaining safety and happiness.[20]

Published in both English and Spanish, the first constitution provided for a limited government that protected individual rights and sought the common welfare. By contrast, the **California Constitution of 1879** would contain class struggle and anti-immigrant animus and encourage the development of the constitution into today's lengthy legal code of over 150 pages, the third-longest constitution in the world. As Gordon Lloyd points out, "There is a degree of public spirit, liberality, civility, and enlightenment in 1849 that is missing from subsequent discourses on the ends of constitutionalism."[21]

The original California Constitution reflected the American founders' document as much as it did the early American state constitutions. We should recall here that the genius of the American Constitution is its unique separation of powers and its dependence on federalism as a means of preserving liberty and providing for energetic yet limited government. Its theoretical principle is the inherent equality of human beings that requires limited government by consent. James Madison's *Federalist* (no. 10, 1787) argued that only a large, commercial democratic republic that fostered deliberation could effectively prevent a majority faction and thus protect the **natural rights** described in the Declaration of Independence—life, liberty, and the pursuit of happiness. In the American founders' view, the smaller the political unit, the more readily an oppressive majority could form. If any governments needed the protection of what Madison called "auxiliary precautions"—such as the separation of powers—it was the state governments. Constitutionally, California exemplifies what the founders feared in state governments and wanted to prevent at the national level.[22] How else could Jefferson's sacred principle—"that though the will of the majority is in all cases to prevail, that will to be rightful must be reasonable; that the minority possess their equal rights, which equal law must protect, and to violate would be oppression"—be preserved?[23] As for the relationship between the U.S. Constitution and the California Constitution, the latter is obviously subordinate to the former by the general principles of federalism; the former's Supremacy Clause (article VI, section 2); and the Fourteenth Amendment, which was ratified in 1868. With the other amendments passed immediately after the Civil War, the Fourteenth Amendment was intended to bring the Constitution into conformity with the Declaration of Independence. The Tenth Amendment does, however, continue to protect a disputed realm of state powers that the federal government may not violate.

Whatever their differences on many vital issues, the American founders agreed that majority rule must follow reason, as embodied in natural rights and constitutionalism. That men and women are born with natural rights means that they have inherent freedoms that no one may violate, without their consent, as expressed in their adoption of constitutional government. These principles may be summed up in the notion that "it is the reason, alone, of the public, that ought to control and regulate the government. The passions ought to be controlled and regulated by the government."[24] To be legitimate, government must obey a rule of reason. The mere possession of power can never justify the choice of a particular policy.

After the Civil War, new conditions led to a new California Constitution. Aided by the completion of the transcontinental railroad in 1869, California's population soared from its early statehood number of 50,000 to about 865,000. No longer primarily a mining economy, the booming new state suffered dramatically from the nationwide depression of the 1870s. The Workingmen's Party blamed the railroads, corporations, and the activities of Central Pacific Railroad's "Big Four" for their miseries.[25] The Big Four were politician Leland Stanford (1824–1893), financier Collis P. Huntington (1821–1900), foreman Charles Crocker (1822–1888), and bookkeeper Mark Hopkins (1814–1878).

The Workingmen's Party struck out as well against the growth of **Chinese immigration**. Known as "Celestials" after the Celestial Empire of China, California's 70,000 or more Chinese—about 8 percent of the population—emigrated to work in the mines and railroads and then sought return to China. In the cities they formed Chinatowns, which were associated with vice. Keep in mind that the Chinese American population during this era was overwhelmingly adult male, and that many of the early Chinese and white female immigrants to California were prostitutes. The constitution of 1879 reflected all these concerns— protecting the people from corrupt politicians, preventing high rates of taxation, overthrowing the power of the corporations (in particular the railroads), and all but expelling the Chinese by restricting their fundamental rights. "Asiatic coolieism is a form of human slavery," the new Constitution declared, while prohibiting employment of Chinese by corporations and the government, discouraging immigration, and encouraging the "removal of Chinese."[26] The Chinese were seen as vice-ridden and unscrupulous competitors with the workingmen. Irish immigrant Denis Kearney, who led a class and anti-Chinese movement, ended his speeches with the refrain, "The Chinese must go!" Mobs attacked Chinatowns and conducted gruesome lynchings of Chinese throughout the state. The respectable establishment of the state was appalled at the violence and sought to establish order, but government by consent can bring only a limited amount of enlightenment, so California's last constitutional convention passed a document that clashed with the U.S. Constitution, federal law, and international treaties. Of course, the state's new constitution and laws had to give way. In response to these legal assaults, the Chinese were not passive victims but fought the discriminatory legislation in courts through their own lawyers, through Chinese counsel, and with the aid of sympathetic whites.[27] "The declaration of your independence, and all the acts of your government, your people, and your history, are against you," contended a Chinese immigrant's 1852 response to the California governor's opposition to the naturalization of his fellows.[28]

Similar questions about ethnic divisions and Americanization arise today, more than a century later. Consider Peter Skerry's reflections on the effect of a heavily bureaucratized, ethnic-focused public policy:

> [T]his style of politics is dependent upon displays of angry protest. But mainly its goals are pursued through quiet bureaucratic and judicial channels, where the racial minority perspective has been thoroughly institutionalized by governmental and foundation elites. Transformations such as that of the Los Angeles County Board of Supervisors will be wrought with little opposition or notice from the public. . . . In essence, this approach is profoundly antipolitical. It teaches those without political power that it can and should be bestowed on them by elite benefactors, whether Anglo or Latino. This approach also transforms Mexican-American leaders into one more voice of principled disharmony and rigidly defined abstracts rights, resistant to compromise in the political arena. In the name of politics, we now have a new source of discord—of antipolitics.[29]

Thus Skerry endorses ethnic politics but not ethnic spoils, a difficult balancing act. In his view, "being a Mexican-American in the Southwest is simply not the same as being a Pole in Chicago."[30] If one is an immigrant, the ability to return to Mexico lessens one's identity with America. Perhaps the major actor in this drama of identity is California higher education: At colleges and universities, the identity politics of race and gender emphasize the place of ethnicity in student lives to an extent that they had never previously faced. Can a person who doesn't speak Spanish be called Latino? Can an ethnic identity forego irregular verbs? An ethnic group that spans the human range of skin, eye, and hair colors can suddenly become nonwhite, a separate race. Skerry points out the example of a Latino police officer in the notorious Rodney King beating, who was routinely described in news reports as white. Skerry also quotes a black community leader who stated that "Latinos can't make up their minds whether they're a minority."[31] Nonetheless, in the view of the media, California reached nonwhite majority status sometime in 2000.[32]

And we Californians, with the rest of America, embrace a diversity of religions—the "new religions of America."[33] For example, this is not the variety present between Protestantism or Orthodoxy, the differences between the Franciscans and the Jesuits in Catholicism, or what distinguishes the branches of Judaism. Buddhists, Hindus, Jains, Muslims, and Sikhs bring a dramatically new way of viewing the sacred—visually expressed in the architecture of their temples, mosques, and other houses of worship. Do these reinforce the American civil religion, which honors the Declaration of Independence and the Constitution and makes America a special nation, or do they transform the nation in unprecedented ways?

We should realize that this task is not simply a sentimental one. Richard Rodriguez critiques multiculturalism:

> I submit that America is not a tale for sentimentalists. . . .
>
> If I am a newcomer to your country, why teach me about my ancestors? I need to know about seventeenth-century Puritans in order to make sense of the rebellion I notice everywhere in the American city. Teach me about mad British kings so I will understand the American penchant for iconoclasm. Then teach me about cowboys and Indians; I should know that tragedies created the country that will create me.[34]

A common education should help make us one people, but sometimes what is learned, especially in one's higher education, makes this unity more difficult to achieve.[35]

So is California remarkably diverse or remarkably uniform for all external appearances, physical and otherwise? Rodriguez maintains there is far more conformity than real diversity, hence the current emphasis on ethnicity. We need not agree with his observation about individualism and ethnicity to appreciate the problem he is pointing to:

> Americans are lonely now. Hispanics and Asians represent to us the alternatives of communal cultures at a time when Americans are demoralized. Americans are no longer sure that economic invincibility derives from individualism.[36]

Above all, we need to see the political significance of these differences.[37] Despite the talk of a nonwhite majority in California (which is

Table 1.1.   California Demographics, 2000

	Race and Ethnicity by Region (%)			
	Los Angeles	San Francisco Bay	Central Valley	Orange/Inland
Asian	12	19	8	8
Black	10	9	5	5
Latino	44	18	25	29
Other	—	—	1	1
White	34	54	61	57

	Voter Registration by Region (%)			
	Los Angeles	San Francisco Bay	Central Valley	Orange/Inland
Democrats	54	53	45	37
Republicans	29	27	41	47
Independents	13	15	10	11
Other parties	4	5	4	5
Registered voters (millions)	3.8	3.3	2.4	2.4

	Political Orientation by Region (%)			
	Los Angeles	San Francisco Bay	Central Valley	Orange/Inland
Liberal	35	36	22	24
Centrist	34	33	36	36
Conservative	31	31	42	40

Source: Mark Baldassare, *California in the New Millenium* (Berkeley: University of California Press, 2000), 143 (on race and ethnicity), 149 (on regions), and 151 (on ideology).

the case only if one counts all Latinos as nonwhite), 76 percent of all likely voters remain non-Latino white. 14 percent are Latino, 6 percent are black, and 4 percent are Asian American. About half of all voters live in Los Angeles County (27 percent) and San Francisco (22 percent).[38] Although the Central Valley is the fastest-growing part of the state, it also remains one of the least populous.

California political views vary, and the causes for this are diverse. They include one's experiences as a member of a racial or ethnic group, but at least as much from the region one lives in, the work one performs, and the views one forms through education. Although geographic location, occupation, race, ethnicity, and income level can all affect one's views on politics, ultimately the individual must consciously determine his or her views, through an examination of the most thoughtful views on politics. Through laziness, ignorance, or indifference, we must not succumb to what Tocqueville called the **tyranny of the majority,** which is the inability or unwillingness to express or even think politically significant thoughts that clash with those of one's peers. "The moral empire of the majority," Tocqueville wrote, "is founded in part on the idea there is more enlightenment and wisdom in many men united than in one alone, in the number of legislators than in their choice. It is the theory of equality applied to intellects."[39] Political correctness is a form of tyranny of the majority, which is a corruption of democracy. Preserving liberty requires work, just as athletic, academic, or any other form of excellence does.

CONCLUSION

California is diverse in numerous ways, geographically and economically as well as by race and ethnicity. The Gold Rush brought about the rapid settlement of California and its entry into the Union under the Compromise of 1850. The constitutional history of California is marked by the steady growth of government under the California Constitution of 1879, which was adopted by the constitutional convention of 1878–1879 under the sway of populist and anti-Chinese demagoguery.

NOTES

1. Alexis de Tocqueville, *Democracy in America*, trans., ed., and with an introduction by Harvey C. Mansfield and Delba Winthrop (Chicago: The University of Chicago Press, 2000), 392. Earlier, in footnote 19 (319), Tocqueville had warned of this problem:

> Something more striking still is taking place in the province of Texas; the state of Texas, as we know, makes up a part of Mexico and serves as its frontier with the United States. For some years, the Anglo-Americans entered individually into this still ill-populated province, bought lands, took possession of industry, and rapidly substituted themselves for the original population. It can be foreseen that if Mexico does not hasten to halt this movement, it will not be long before Texas escapes from it.

2. Tocqueville, *Democracy*, 190.
3. Victor Davis Hanson, *The Land Was Everything* (New York: The Free Press, 2000), 24–25.
4. Kevin Starr, *Material Dreams: Southern California through the 1920s* (New York: Oxford University Press, 1990), 69.

5. Richard Rodriguez, *Days of Obligation: Arguments with My Mexican Father* (New York: Viking, 1992), 28.

6. Starr, *Material Dreams*, 3.

7. Barry Turner, ed., *The Statesman's Yearbook 2001* (London: Macmillan, 2001), 1725. This annual compilation of descriptive and statistical information about the "politics, cultures, and economies of the world" (including each American state) gives a succinct five-page overview of California that, while uneven in the detail presented, makes an excellent brief introduction. Other basic information can be found on California's website: <www.ca.gov/state/portal/myca_homepage.jsp> (accessed 26 December 2001).

8. Rodriguez, *Days of Obligation*, 169.

9. Rodriguez, *Days*, 63–64.

10. Particularly damaging for students who might otherwise comprehend the greatness of the Founding Fathers is the disputable notion that they were racist, sexist, and classist. For a defense of the founders against such criticism, see Thomas G. West, *Vindicating the Founders: Race, Sex, Class, and Justice in the Origins of America* (Lanham, Md.: Rowman & Littlefield, 1997).

11. James Madison, *The Federalist*, no. 10 (1787).

12. For a insightful study of George Washington's farewell address, see Matthew Spalding and Patrick Garrity, *A Sacred Union of Citizens: George Washington's Farewell Address and the American Character*, introduction by Daniel J. Boorstin, (Lanham, Md.: Rowman & Littlefield, 1996).

13. See Harry V. Jaffa, *Crisis of the House Divided: An Interpretation of the Issues in the Lincoln-Douglas Debates* (Chicago: University of Chicago Press, 1982, originally published, Oxford University Press, 1959); and Harry V. Jaffa, *A New Birth of Freedom: Abraham Lincoln and the Coming of the Civil War* (Lanham, Md.: Rowman & Littlefield, 2000).

14. Aristotle, *The Politics of Aristotle*, ed. Peter L. Phillips Simpson (Chapel Hill: University of North Carolina, 1997), book I. This is the best edition for students.

15. Abraham Lincoln, Address, "Address Before the Wisconsin State Agricultural Society, Milwaukee, Wisconsin," September 30, 1859, in *Collected Works*, vol. 3 (New Brunswick: Rutgers University Press, 1953), 471–72.

16. Malcolm J. Rohrbough, *Days of Gold: The California Gold Rush and the American Nation* (Berkeley: University of California Press, 1997), 2. Alexander Hamilton's son, William Stephen Hamilton, died in August 1850 in Sacramento. Jefferson might have sneered at his pursuit of gold, but Alexander Hamilton might have approved, and those differences sum up the new America that arose through the enormous changes, or emphases, gold brought about. Tocqueville compares the westward movement of Americans to "what happened at the fall of the Roman Empire" (*Democracy*, 269). What might he have said about the Gold Rush! See also Kevin Starr, *Americans and the California Dream, 1850–1915* (New York: Oxford University Press, 1973), 54.

17. James Bryce, *The American Commonwealth*, vol. 2, (Indianapolis: Liberty Fund Press, 1995), 1066.

18. The Gold Rush camps, though often enough scenes of violence, managed to produce an order based on commonsense property rights. According to journalist

and activist Carey McWilliams, the miners sought to "safeguard the equality of opportunity which had prevailed at the outset." In addition to barring slavery, other measures were taken to insure equality and to limit the size of each claim. See Carey McWilliams, *California: The Great Exception* (Berkeley: University of California, 1949; reprinted 1999, with foreword by Lewis H. Lapham), 28. For analyses by economists, see Terry L. Anderson and P. J. Hill, "An American Experiment in Anarcho-Capitalism: the *Not* So Wild, Wild West," *The Journal of Libertarian Studies* 3, no. 1 (Spring 1979), 9–28; and "The Evolution of Property Rights: A Study of the American West," *The Journal of Law and Economics* 28, no. 1, (April 1975), 163–179.

19. Herman Belz, "Popular Sovereignty, The Right of Revolution, and California Statehood," *Nexus: A Journal of Opinion* 6 (Spring 2001), 3–22.

20. California Constitution, art. I, sec. 1 (1849). Currently this article, as revised on November 5, 1974, reads: "All people are by nature free and independent and have inalienable rights. Among these are enjoying and defending life and liberty, acquiring, possessing, and protecting property, and pursuing and obtaining safety, happiness, *and privacy*" (italics added).

21. Gordon Lloyd, "Nature and Convention in the Creation of the 1849 California Constitution," *Nexus: A Journal of Opinion* 6 (Spring 2001), 38.

22. James Madison, *The Federalist,* nos. 10 (1787) and 51 (1788).

23. Thomas Jefferson, Address, "First Inaugural Address," March 4, 1801, in Merrill Peterson, ed., *Jefferson* (New York: Library of America, 1984), 492–93.

24. Madison, *The Federalist,* no. 49 (1788).

25. For a positive view of the railroads and the men who made them, from the Big Four to the Chinese immigrants, see Stephen E. Ambrose, *Nothing Like It in the World: The Men Who Built the Transcontinental Railroad 1863–1869* (New York: Simon & Schuster, 2000), 17. Ambrose describes the transcontinental railroad—he does not discuss California's Central Pacific Railroad—as "the greatest achievement of the American people in the nineteenth century," surpassed only by the Civil War and the abolition of slavery.

26. California Constitution, art. XIX, sec. 1, sec. 4 (1879).

27. Charles J. McClain, *In Search of Equality: The Chinese Struggle Against Discrimination in Nineteenth-Century America* (Berkeley: University of California Press, 1994). More on the Chinese and other ethnic groups will appear in chapter 2.

28. McClain, *In Search,* 12.

29. Peter Skerry, *Mexican-Americans: The Ambivalent Minority* (New York: Free Press, 1993), 377–378. See also Samuel Huntington, "The Special Case of Mexican Immigration: Why Mexico Is a Problem," *The American Enterprise* (December 2000), 22. Huntington wrote, "Mexican immigration looms as a unique and disturbing challenge to our cultural integrity, our national identity, and potentially to our future as a country."

30. Peter Skerry, "Mexican Immigration Is Different," *The American Enterprise* (December 2000), 22.

31. Skerry, *Mexican-Americans,* 9–10.

32. Books on race and identity abound. Two standard authors are Lawrence H. Fuchs, *The American Kaleidoscope: Race, Ethnicity, and the Civic Culture* (Han-

over: University Press of New England, 1990); and Nathan Glazer, *We Are All Multiculturalists Now* (Cambridge, Mass.: Harvard University Press, 1997). A wide variety of articles may be found in Stephan Thernstrom, ed., *The Harvard Encyclopedia of American Ethnic Groups* (Cambridge, Mass.: Harvard University Press, 1980).

33. See Diana L. Eck's fulsome account in *A New Religious America: How a "Christian Country" Has Become the World's Most Religiously Diverse Nation* (San Francisco: Harper San Francisco, 2001).

34. Rodriguez, *Days*, 169.

35. Skerry, *Mexican Americans*, 362–365.

36. Rodriguez, *Days*, 171.

37. All tables are reprinted from Mark Baldassare, *California in the New Millennium* (Berkeley: University of California Press, 2000), 143, 149, and 151.

38. See the Public Policy Institute of California website: <www.ppic.org/facts/likelyvote.mar01.pdf> (accessed 26 December 2001).

39. Tocqueville, *Democracy*, 236.

Chapter Two

Constitutional Government in California: The Evolution of a Progressive State

> Democratic peoples often hate the depositories of the central power; but they always love this power itself. . . . I have shown that equality suggests to men the thought of a lone, uniform, and strong government. I have just brought out that it gives them the taste for it; the nations of our day tend therefore toward a government of this kind. . . . I think that in the democratic centuries that are going to open up, individual independence and local liberties will always be the product of art. Centralization will be the natural government.[1]

The great national reform movement known as **Progressivism** sought to replace fundamental American political practices, such as a limited government of separated powers, with an unlimited government closer to the parliamentary model. It drew its principles from Jean-Jacques Rousseau (1712–1778) and his German followers such as G. W. F. Hegel (1770–1831), who make the will of the people the source of all legitimate rule. Because the will of the people cannot contradict itself, it cannot be limited, and hence powers should not be separated as they are in American democracy. This will is not simply a spontaneous outburst, but is self-knowing and self-actualizing. Its discipline is found in the administrative state, popularly known as "the bureaucracy." The core of this European philosophy found its way into the beliefs of prominent American Progressives such as the prolific John Dewey (1859–1952). For such Americans, Progressivism stood for a scientific attitude toward politics, which explicitly rejected the natural rights basis of American politics as expressed in documents such as the Declaration of Independence. This meant that there were no inherent limits on legitimate government, as in the founding principle of just government requiring the

17

consent of the governed. The Progressives were particularly critical of property rights–based arguments that corporate America was fond of using, so government regulation, in the name of the public interest, followed logically. Early Progressives also despised the machine politics of their era. The political machine, the spoils system, and the vibrancy of American politics received an immortal defense in the classic *Plunkitt of Tammany Hall: A Series of Very Plain Talks on Very Practical Politics,* in which George Washington Plunkitt protested that the reform movement was "underminin' the manhood of the nation and makin' the Declaration of Independence a farce."[2]

The administrative state, staffed by experts from the universities (reform politics' great ally), would take on the challenge of an industrializing society now being filled with new waves of immigrants. Progressivist politics was closely aligned with developing academic programs in the universities, especially the new discipline of political science. Evolutionary science such as the important work of Charles Darwin allegedly swept away the claims of self-evident truths of the founding generation, which rested on the notion of a knowable and enduring human nature. The will of the new political-academic elite sought to satisfy the people's security and needs.

In foreign policy, Progressivism could manifest itself in imperialism, such as American involvement in the Philippines during the Spanish-American War; in isolationism, as seen in the policies of California politician **Hiram Johnson;** or in idealist internationalism, as seen in President Woodrow Wilson (1913–1921). In California, Progressivism would adopt a hostile nativist stance, opposing Asian immigration and supporting discriminatory legislation. Contemporary liberalism certainly embodies many tenets of Progressivism, as we see in much Great Society legislation. But liberalism has also advanced a host of class, gender, and race-oriented domestic policy views beyond the Progressive agenda.[3]

Perhaps Progressivism's clearest sign of the reliance on an enlightened electorate are the initiative and referendum. These are means by which the electorate can directly vote in new laws or, in the case of California, amend the state constitution. (The mechanics of the initiative and referendum are discussed in chapter 5's coverage of campaigns and elections.)

In California, as well as in other states, Progressivism aimed at transforming both Democratic and Republican parties into its image of a reformed politics, one free of bosses and partisanship. For example, the Big Four's railroad dominated the economy of the state and whatever laws and judges were needed to maintain its grip.[4] Regulation of powerful industries such as railroads (although, in principle, this applied to any economic entity) was also deemed necessary to support the public interest.

Progressivism was not a labor or agriculture party, as sprouted up in other regions of the country. It was far more a party of middle-class respectability, born in the Midwest and with roots in New England religion.[5] Though many Progressive politicians were lawyers and journalists, many others were reform-minded businessmen who were labeled "goo-goos" for their good-government enthusiasms. Perhaps a character in Frank Norris's novel, *The Octopus,* best expresses the frustrations of the reformers: "California likes to be fooled. . . . Indifference to public affairs—absolute indifference, it stamps us all. Our state is the very paradise of fakirs."[6]

G. Alan Tarr summarizes Progressivism's early political achievements: "The most striking illustration of [them]. . . was the set of amendments adopted in California in 1911 that established a railroad commission to regulate all public utilities, revised the tax system to shift more of the burden to corporations and banks, and provided for employers' liability, a minimum wage, and enhanced powers of eminent domain."[7] But Progressivism's reformist, anti-corporation rhetoric fueled more radical parties, even as it robbed them of adherents.

California's principal Progressive politician was Hiram Johnson, who came to prominence as a crusading attorney. He investigated the Southern Pacific Railroad and, in emotional speeches, denounced its control over the economy of the state. This "short and stocky" Republican became the dominant figure in California politics, serving continuously as governor from 1910 to 1917 and thereafter as a U.S. senator until his death in 1945.[8] He was so popular that he often captured both major parties' nominations. He was also nominated vice president for Theodore Roosevelt's Bull Moose Party in 1912, losing by a large margin to Woodrow Wilson but getting more electoral college and popular votes than Republican incumbent William Howard Taft. Johnson later sought the presidency, but this proud man would reject Harding's offer of the vice presidency on the Republican ticket in 1920.

Under Johnson's leadership California adopted the initiative, referendum, and recall, thus injecting direct democracy into its politics. His support of cross-filing (the ability to capture both the Democratic and Republican nominations for the same office, as mentioned above), local and judicial nonpartisanship, workmen's compensation, and women's suffrage were his other notable Progressive achievements,[9] and he envisioned other reforms. As explained by John Aubrey Douglass, the Progressive reform of higher education "would provide a caste of trained labor and professionals, a source of culture and research that would build a more learned, competent, and productive society capable of wisely using these new democratic powers."[10]

Perhaps the temperamental Johnson's significance can be explained in terms of a far better known national figure, former Chief Justice of the United States Supreme Court **Earl Warren.** Warren (1891–1974) was one of California's most renowned and controversial political figures. He served as California's attorney general (1939–1942) and thrice as its governor (1942–1953). Following his 1948 nomination for vice president, in which he ran with Republican New York Governor Thomas Dewey unsuccessfully against Harry Truman and Alban Barkley, he was appointed by President Dwight Eisenhower as Chief Justice of the Supreme Court (1954–1969). He wrote the *Brown v. Board of Education* school desegregation decision of 1954, the reapportionment cases, and numerous other court decisions expanding civil liberties, but his most important contribution was to make the Court and other courts, federal and state, conscious political reformers. In this sense, Warren was an archetypal Progressive in his belief in active government and subsequent disdain for the separation of powers. Warren declared that he

> believed in the progressivism of Hiram Johnson, who had broken the power of the predatory interests by opening up our state and local governments so the people could govern themselves through free elections. . . . I was committed to the nonpartisanship he brought into city and county government. I believed in the civil service he established, putting an end to the spoils system of former days and enabling public employees to live without fear of discharge merely because of a change in administration. . . .
>
> I believed implicitly in the direct primary for all state and local offices, and in the cross-filing procedure for partisan state offices. These were reforms that made it possible for an impecunious young man like myself to launch on a public career that would last half a century. They sounded the death knell of the old-fashioned political boss.[11]

As we have seen, the late chief justice was fond of the practice of cross-filing. Pulitzer Prize–winning historian Don Fehrenbacher and his coauthor Norman Tutorow comment that cross-filing favored the incumbent and "also blurred party lines, undermined party responsibility, and gave California politics a peculiar cast of irrationality."[12] By favoring incumbency and implicitly giving more power to unelected elites such as new political bosses replacing the old, cross-filing aided the Progressivist cause. Such was the dominance of the Progressive Republicans that the first Democrat to capture the gubernatorial seat in the twentieth century was Cuthbert Olson, who served only one term (1939–1943).

Another prominent Republican Progressive went on to the presidency—Herbert Hoover, who never held elected office before his presidency (1929–1933), but was President Harding's Secretary of Commerce and had arranged food relief for a post–World War I starving Europe. He was a citizen who served, a nonpartisan enlightened administrator, and the very model of a Progressive anti-politician. While Progressivism flourished primarily within the Republican Party, it also had its influence on the Democrats and on radical movements. The rejection of natural rights in favor of an evolution of ever-expanding benefits would be seen in its Depression-Era extreme in Upton Sinclair's Eliminate Poverty in California (EPIC) movement, together with the Townsend Plan to give the elderly a monthly subsidy. Sinclair, author of *The Jungle* and a long-time socialist, surprised all observers by winning the Democratic nomination for governor in 1934. His nomination and other Depression-Era measures, such as the Townsend Plan and the Ham-and-Eggs Initiative, exemplified the enduring vitality of the 1879 Constitution. These radical proposals would have given the elderly scrip worth a disproportionate amount of money that had to be spent within a specific time period. Though Sinclair and his fantastic major proposals were defeated, the principle of direct majority rule that could drastically alter life remained.[13]

While they were both keen partisans, California Republican Richard Nixon and Democrat Edmund G. "Pat" Brown exhibited Progressivism as well: Nixon in his willingness to centralize the government to carry out reforms, and Brown in his expansion of the University of California system. Though a conservative, Ronald Reagan benefited from his image as a "citizen-legislator," who would come in from the outside and reform a corrupt system. Thus he, too, made use of Progressive imagery.[14]

The legacy of Progressivism remains in the California Constitution as we know it today. The Constitution's sprawl—it is the world's third longest after India's and Louisiana's—is illustrated by the diversity of its contents, which combine language from the American founding era with details about state retirement benefits.[15] Amended over 500 times since 1879, the constitution has become a complex code and a basic law for Californians. As the state's own edition of the institutions of its government puts it:

The fundamental difference between the California Constitution and the Constitution of the United States is that the Federal Constitution is a grant of
power to Congress and is also a limitation upon its powers, whereas the State
Constitution is a limitation upon the power of the State Legislature. . . . The
sphere of state activity is more extensive than that of the federal government
since its powers are original and inherent, not derived or delegated, as are the
powers of the federal government.[16]

Californians continue to live under the constitution's attempts to regulate corporate power.[17] We will discuss selected provisions of the constitution in the chapters that follow.

Reflecting the frustrations of many citizens, a 1994 Constitution Revision Commission attempted to make California government more "efficient." Dissenters protested that the commission's streamlining
proposals would accelerate the Progressivist tendencies that had created
the current problem of centralized administration.[18] The Progressives'
intellectual arm, the universities and think tanks, has proposed more
radical reforms such as a unicameral legislature, while strengthening the
separation of powers by a more consolidated executive.[19] Intended to
purify politics, term limits is a Progressive measure favored by significant
numbers in both parties. Party identification is prohibited for all but a
few major state offices, and parties may not endorse nonpartisan candidates. The voters' natural, healthy suspicion of parties has led to the further weakening of the party system. This in turn accelerates the
centralization that Tocqueville feared, which favors those least subject
to the political process (the courts and the bureaucracy) over the elected
branches and especially the bicameral legislature and local governments.
The current California Constitution shows that the Progressive attacks
on corrupt politics are fundamentally attacks on political activity generally. Whatever their original intent, Progressivism's practices have made
it more difficult to protest the increasing reach of the administrative state
that is Progressivism's hitherto highest achievement. Thus, it is far too
modest for George Mowry to conclude, "The Progressive supplied an
honest and decent middle way between a corrupt labor party and a corrupt corporation-dominated government."[20]

The enemies of Progressivism are as diverse as its friends, as is the case
with any form of populism—once one sees the elites claiming to be the
voice of the people. Whatever later mitigation of the treatment of the
Chinese, the principal change had occurred—the rejection of limited
government and its natural rights basis—and would continue to guide
the politics of California. In the view of some, the spirit of Kearney, and
not the deliberation of the earlier constitutional convention, would

guide California politics. But others would defend at least instances of majoritarian governance. Though a staunch critic of unlimited democracy, Edward J. Erler contends, "It is simply to confuse form with substance to argue that . . . the people are incapable of comprehending anything but appeals to passions and prejudices."[21]

Erler is highlighting the consequences and dilemmas of Progressivism that California exemplifies and with which we still struggle today. Are Progressivism and its innovations enemies or allies of self-government? Has Progressivism itself become a house divided that might even bring itself down? Certainly critics of the initiative and referendum, such as noted journalist Peter Schrag, take this view: He maintains that these devices have fueled "the rabid antigovernment fervor of the early nineties."[22] He would point to Proposition 13, which rolled back and limited increases in property taxes; Proposition 187, which restricted illegal immigrants' rights; and Proposition 209, which prohibited race and gender preferences by state government, including public education admissions and hiring. It is a telling point that Proposition 209, the California Civil Rights Initiative, won by a 55–45 percent margin at the same time that Democrat Bill Clinton defeated Republican Bob Dole by a 51–38 percent margin. 58 percent of white women and 66 percent of white men supported Proposition 209, but three-fourths of blacks and Latinos and 61 percent of Asians opposed it.[23]

Regardless of how one stands on the contentious issue of race, ethnic, and gender preferences, one wonders why representative government, with its spirit of deliberation and compromise, might not be a better means of deciding such issues, rather than up-and-down votes. Yet, one might also counter that some issues are of sufficiently general principle that a popular vote on them would reflect a political spirit that a democracy can ill afford to lose. One might consider both these standpoints when examining the controversial Proposition 22, which bans homosexual marriages.

CONCLUSION

The 1879 constitution, which eliminated the restraints of the constitution of 1849, provided for regulation of economic life and led the way for the Progressive Era reforms of Governor (and later Senator) Hiram Johnson. On a national level, Progressivism sought to alter fundamental constitutional principles such as federalism and the separation of powers. Progressives wished to restrain what they regarded as corrupt practices by political parties, especially when these parties favored private interests such as railroads and the emerging corporations. Progressive reforms sought to weaken political parties and strengthen an administrative state comprised of rational, scientific administrators. Of use in bypassing or replacing legislators are the initiative, referendum, and recall. Republicans Johnson and Earl Warren remain the most prominent Progressive politicians in California history.

Other Californians who come from the Progressive tradition include Herbert Hoover, Pat Brown, and Richard Nixon. Others who deviated from Progressivism, yet benefited in ways from it, were socialist Upton Sinclair and conservative Ronald Reagan. Suspicion toward politicians and political parties remains a major feature of California political life that had its most rigorous expression in Progressivism, and the current constitution illustrates this antipolitical attitude. When applied to today's diverse California, the administrative state of the Progressive legacy encourages ethnic and racial divisions as a means of keeping politicians from those groups in power.

NOTES

1. Alexis de Tocqueville, *Democracy in America*, trans., ed., and with an introduction by Harvey C. Mansfield and Delba Winthrop (Chicago: The University of Chicago Press, 2000), 644–645.

2. George Washington Plunkitt, as recorded by William L. Riordon, *Plunkitt of Tammany Hall* (New York: E. P. Dutton, 1963), 39. The conversations of Boss Plunkitt with journalist Riordan were originally published in 1905 and contained chapters whose titles include "Honest Graft and Dishonest Graft," "Dangers of the Dress Suit in Politics," and "Bosses Preserve the Nation."

3. Primary texts for understanding Progressivism include Herbert Croly, *The Promise of American Life* (New York: Capricorn, 1964, originally published 1909); Charles Beard, *An Economic Interpretation of the Constitution of the United States* (New York: Macmillan, 1913); and the works of John Dewey, especially *The Public and Its Problems* (Chicago: Swallow Press, 1927). As leading Progressive Era scholar Eldon Eisenach notes, these thinkers are derivative in many ways from earlier, far more obscure figures in economics, history, law, and the new discipline of sociology. See *The Lost Promise of Progressivism* (Lawrence, Kans.: The University Press of Kansas, 1994). For an academic critique of Progressivism, see Thomas Silver, *Coolidge and the Historians* (Durham, N.C.: Carolina Academic Press, 1982).

4. See George E. Mowry, *The California Progressives* (Chicago: Quadrangle, 1963; originally published by University of California Press, 1951), 12. Perhaps too cynically, Mowry contended that for all the power of the railroad, the state "corrupted itself." If it weren't the railroad, he believed, it would have been something else.

5. Mowry, *California Progressives,* 87–91.

6. Frank Norris, *The Octopus: A Story of California* (New York: New American Library, Signet Classics, 1964; originally published 1901), 215. *The Octopus* is a novel based on contemporary California events, in which callous railroad owners destroy the lives of decent, hardworking ranchers, farmers, and immigrants.

7. G. Alan Tarr, *Understanding State Constitutions* (Princeton: Princeton University Press, 1998), 148.

8. Mowry, *California Progressives,* 113–116. Mowry does not paint an appealing portrait: This reformer appears to fulfill virtually every cliché about a hack politician. Not an intellectual nor a cultured man, he was "a sensitive and thin-skinned rebel . . . nervous, moody, and insecure." A barely more generous appraisal is provided in Spencer C. Olin, Jr., *California's Prodigal Sons: Hiram Johnson and the Progressives 1911–1917* (Berkeley: University of California Press, 1968), 96–99.

9. For Johnson's achievements, see Mowry, *California Progressives;* and Olin, *Prodigal Sons.* These terms are discussed in this and later chapters.

10. John Aubrey Douglass, *The California Idea and American Higher Education* (Stanford: Stanford University Press, 2000), 82.

11. Earl Warren, *The Memoirs of Chief Justice Earl Warren* (Garden City, N.Y.: Doubleday & Co., 1977), 171.

12. *California: An Illustrated History* (New York: D. Van Nostrand Co., 1968), 97.

13. See, among others, Kevin Starr, *Endangered Dreams: The Great Depression in California* (New York: Oxford University Press, 1996). For a general history of California that emphasizes leftist radicals' influence on the development of politics and culture, see Stephen Schwartz, *From West to East: California and the Making of the American Mind* (New York: Free Press, 1998). For the evolution of Progressivism to liberalism on the national level, see the work of Sidney M. Milkis, particularly *The President and the Parties: The Transformation of the American Party System Since the New Deal* (New York: Oxford University Press, 1993).

14. Steven Hayward, "Ronald Reagan and the Transformation of Modern California," *Nexus: A Journal of Opinion* 6 (Spring 2001): 145–156; John J. Pitney, "Nixon, California, and American Politics," *Nexus: A Journal of Opinion* 6 (Spring 2001): 133–144; and Steven Hayward, *The Age of Reagan, 1964–1980: The Fall of the Old Liberal Order* (New York: Prima Publishing, 2001).

15. Article IX, section 1, on education, reads, "A general diffusion of knowledge and intelligence being essential to the preservation of the rights and liberties of the people, the Legislature shall encourage by all suitable means the promotion of intellectual, scientific, moral, and agricultural improvement." Compare this with the Northwest Ordinance's pre-Constitutional declaration: "Religion, morality, and knowledge, being necessary to good government and the happiness of mankind, schools and the means of education shall forever be encouraged." Northwest Ordinance, article 3, in *Documents of American History,* ed. Henry Steele Commager (Englewood Cliffs, N.J.: Prentice-Hall, 1973), 131.

16. E. Dotson Wilson and Brian S. Ebbert, *California's Legislature* (Sacramento: California State Legislature, Office of the Chief Clerk of the Assembly, 1998), 16.

17. The relationship between the two constitutions has become more complicated

in recent years. In 1965 the California Supreme Court invented a new doctrine of "independent state grounds," an attempt to confine questions that are covered in federal case law to state courts when the state constitution has language similar to that of the U.S. Constitution. Thus a Californian could have more rights as a state citizen (for example, as a criminal defendant) than he or she might have in the federal courts as a U.S. citizen. For more on this theme, see chapter 8, "The California Courts and the Progressive Legacy."

18. California Constitution Revision Commission, "Opposing Views," in *Final Report and Recommendations to the Governor and the Legislature* (Sacramento: State of California, 1996), 85–98.

19. See Bruce E. Cain and Roger G. Noll, eds., *Constitutional Reform in California* (Berkeley: Institute of Governmental Studies Press, 1995).

20. Mowry, *California Progressives*, 301.

21. Edward J. Erler, "Californians and Their Constitution: Progressivism, Direct Democracy, and the Administrative State," *Nexus: A Journal of Opinion* 6 (Spring 2001): 252.

22. Peter Schrag, *Paradise Lost: California's Experience, America's Future* (Berkeley: University of California Press, 1998), 271.

23. For a balanced insider account of this struggle, see Lydia Chavez, *The Color Bind: California's Battle to End Affirmative Action* (Berkeley: University of California Press, 1998). Chairman Ward Connerly of the Proposition 209 campaign subsequently wrote a moving autobiography, *Creating Equal: My Fight Against Race Preferences* (San Francisco: Encounter Books, 2000).

Chapter Three

Public Opinion and the Media

The majority, being an absolute master in making the law and in overseeing its execution, having equal control over those who govern and over those who are governed, regards public officials as its passive agents and willingly deposits in them the care of serving its designs. . . .[1]

Journalists in the United States, therefore, in general hardly have an elevated position; their education is only sketchy, and the turn of their ideas is often vulgar. . . . The spirit of the journalist in America is to attack coarsely, without preparation and without art, the passions of those whom it addresses, to set aside principles in order to grab men, to follow them into their private lives, and to lay bare their weaknesses and their vices.[2]

The United States is ruled by public opinion in the most fundamental sense. This is also true of California. With modern polling techniques, political leaders can maintain a daily vigil over the ebbs and flows of opinion. This chapter provides an explanation of the basic components of public opinion. However, the conditions for a healthy republic require something other than a voracious majoritarianism fed by the establishment media. For a republic to survive, the deliberative sense of the public must rule instead of its unfettered will.[3] We will also examine the nature of the media in state politics and how it has changed over the years.

PUBLIC OPINION

The most important measurement of public opinion occurs on election days. Voters cast ballots for individuals seeking a particular office and for initiatives, referenda, or recalls. In the interim period between elections, public opinion is most commonly measured by public opinion polls, although direct contact with voters is still important.[4] The basic components of public opinion are salience effects, attention cycles, and liberal and conservative ideologies, along with public opinion polls and their findings.

Salience Effects

There is no such thing as *a* public opinion. Public opinion is divided into various segments, and its two major segments are the **mass public** and the **elite public**.[5] These categories do not automatically apply to levels of income or social status, but are determined by a person's knowledge of and interest in a particular issue. For example, consider the issue area of safety regulations for highway construction workers. A millionaire who works in a high-rise office building will not necessarily be an expert on road construction, and is probably just as ignorant as most other people are concerning highway construction safety. A highway construction worker, on the other hand, is quite knowledgeable about the subject. On this particular issue, therefore, a political leader might very well recognize the construction worker—with plenty of coworkers who might feel compelled to express their pleasure or displeasure at the next election— as part of the elite and the millionaire as part of the mass public.

The relative interest of mass and elite publics determines the saliency of an issue. The more salient the issue, the more likely a political leader is to follow public opinion. The less salient the issue, the more likely a political leader is to interject his or her private opinions. An issue has the highest level of salience when both segments of public opinion, mass and elite, are aware of the problem and are prepared to act on their opinions. On these high-salience issues, an officeholder or candidate is under great pressure to support the position held by the majority, no matter what his or her private opinion might be. The most prominent examples of high-salience issues are taxes, the economy, and education.

Issues that rouse the elite public but not the mass public are identified as medium-salience issues. On such issues, a political leader has a difficult choice. On the one hand, the mass public has little knowledge or interest in the issue and the political leader might see an opportunity to employ some independent judgment. On the other hand, the intensity of elite opinion might outweigh their lack of numbers. Examples of medium-salience issues include tobacco taxes, state bond issues, and public works projects.

Issues in which neither the elite nor the mass public is interested are known as low-salience issues. On such issues the officeholder or candidate has, for the most part, a free hand to take a position. Examples of low-salience issues include technical budget matters and government reorganization. However, one must keep in mind that the salience of an issue is not the same as the importance of an issue. An issue of low salience, such as a budget item, may be extremely important and very expensive yet fail to provoke public interest.

Attention Cycles

Public interest in a particular issue is often cyclical. Political scientists refer to this phenomenon as the **attention cycle,**[6] which has three stages: The first is the crisis stage. An elected official, interest group leader, or media figure attempts to bring attention to a particular issue by labeling it as a crisis. In order to do this, the crisis entrepreneur will need to get the attention of the media. This is usually accomplished by a press conference at which a victim of some sort will recount his or her personal story to the press. Soon enough, there will be talk of a social security crisis, prescription drug crisis, or gun violence crisis.[7]

Some issues fade quickly after the crisis stage. However, a select few may gain the attention of a significant number of policymakers and make it to the second stage, legislative consideration. Such issues then become the topic of legislative hearings and gubernatorial workshops. Next, a wide variety of proposed plans leading to specific bills are introduced into the legislature.[8] The symbolic rhetoric of the crisis stage is transformed into the technical legislative language of the second stage.

Once an issue has made it into actual legislation, it enters the third and final stage. Either one of three things will occur: 1) the crisis passes, 2) the public comes to the opinion that the cure would be worse than the disease and the legislation dies, or 3) the issue is passed into law. The first two scenarios are the most common; rarely do issues maintain public interest long enough to become law. Very often, issues will reappear year after year, only to suffer the same fate. Elected officials are quite aware of the fickle nature of public opinion and of the need to stick to a few broad legislative goals with easily identifiable themes in order to succeed.

As we will see regarding the California legislature in chapter 6, our policy system is designed to frustrate the efforts of policymakers who rely on emotive rhetoric. The founders of this country wanted their government to reflect the careful consideration of the people, not their momentary desires. On this point, even California's progressive constitution allows for some filtering to take place. Major changes in the law are most likely to take place only if the public is willing to devote a significant amount of attention to it over an extended period of time.[9]

Conservatives and Liberals

Another common way in which public opinion is examined is by studying political ideologies.[10] The most fundamental ideological division in public opinion is that between conservatives and liberals. What do these terms mean?

The modern American conservative believes in the traditional ideas of individual freedom and responsibility. Such freedom and responsibility are not dangerous to the conservative because American conservatism, if understood properly, is derived from the idea that all human beings share an equal nature, an ability to make decisions based upon a common-sense morality. This is the fundamental idea of human equality that is at the heart of the American regime. Liberalism, at its core, denies that such a common-sense morality exists and, even if such a morality were to exist, doubts the average person's ability to understand it. Therefore, a large administrative state is required to regulate even the most mundane aspects of private and public life. American conservatives take the position that they are "conserving" the traditions of the American founding. American liberalism takes the position that such traditions are restrictive, hence the need to be "liberated" from them.[11]

However, it cannot be said that conservatives favor less government and liberals favor more. Because the two ideologies are derived from fundamentally different views of human nature, each ideology calls for different kinds of government action in different cases. For example, a liberal is likely to be in favor of gun control but against the death penalty, while a conservative is likely to be against gun control yet in favor of the death penalty. A liberal is likely to see gun control as a necessary government restriction to prevent citizens from acting unreasonably in self-protection or otherwise. On the other hand, a liberal is likely to see the death penalty as a residual institution based upon old-fashioned ideas of justice derived from moral absolutes that may not be relevant to a particular case.

In contrast, a conservative is likely to see the death penalty, properly administered, as an execution of a rational system of justice that is understandable to the average citizen: appropriate punishment for a particular crime. This same logic leads the conservative to be opposed to gun control; rational creatures existing in a rational world should be able to make sensible decisions regarding their own protection.

Public Opinion Polling

It is the job of the political pollster to collect accurate readings of public opinions. To do this, the pollster must undertake a scientific poll, which has two main components: an appropriate **sample** and a **stratified random distribution**.[12]

California has over 30 million people; therefore, it would be impossible to ask every single Californian their opinion on a certain issue. However, a pollster can gain an estimate of the public's opinion by sampling, in which he or she takes a sample of the population, then measures the public's opinions on certain matters. When constructing a sample, the pollster's main concern is to eliminate **bias** from the sample. For example, suppose you wanted to measure the most popular baseball franchise in the state but you only conducted a sample in San Francisco and Marin Counties. Chances are that an overwhelming number of people would say the San Francisco Giants. This poll is biased to the extent that the sample is not reflective of California's overall population.

One method of eliminating bias is to select people for a sample on a random basis, such as a random selection of all the telephone numbers in the state. However, a good pollster will do more than just construct a random sample. A truly scientific sample will use a stratified random distribution so that the demographic characteristics of the sample are similar to those of the population. An unbiased sample would be one that takes a proportionate amount of people from the various regions of the state, allowing for differences in race, gender, and estimated income levels. If a stratified random distribution is used, a poll can accurately measure the nature of public opinion in California from a sample of 500–3,000 people.

Most public opinion polls are either phone surveys or exit polls. Phone surveys are conducted year-round, and exit polls take place only on election days. Various polling firms hire people to ask voters a series of questions as they exit the location at which they cast their ballots. Of course, participation in any survey is strictly voluntary, which may affect findings.

Recent Findings

Californians differ on a variety of issues across a number of dimensions. There can be differences of opinion on an issue according to partisanship, ideology, gender, or age, among others. Consider the findings in table 3.1, which compare California public opinion between Democrats,

Democracy in California

Table 3.1. Rank of Issue Importance by Party Registration and Political Ideology

	Party		Ideology	
Issue	*Republican*	*Democrat*	*Conservative*	*Liberal*
Public Schools	1	1	1	2
Crime	2	18	4	17
Illegal Drugs	3	12	1	26
Healthcare Costs	4	1	5	1
Illegal Immigration	5	23	1	28
Electricity Costs	6	14	7	19
Taxes	7	19	5	27
Higher Education	7	8	8	5
Job Creation	9	11	14	11
Electricity Supply	10	21	10	10
State Economy	11	19	11	14
Terrorism and Security	12	14	13	22
State Budget Deficit	12	25	11	24
Public Health System	14	3	15	2
Cost of Living	15	7	8	12
Traffic Congestion	16	16	15	15
Gun Control	17	9	17	7
Housing Costs	18	12	18	10
Air and Water Pollution	19	5	21	9
Population Growth	20	22	23	17
Abortion	21	27	18	23
Water Supply	21	16	24	12
Welfare	23	23	22	19
Unemployment	24	9	20	8
Protecting Environment	25	4	26	4
Poverty	26	5	25	6
Race Relations	27	26	28	24
Government Services	28	27	28	24

Source: Field poll, February 2000 (Mark DeCamillo, director): <field.com/fieldpollonline/subscribers/COT-02-Feb-Issues.pdf> (accessed 4 May 2002).
Note: Ties are possible; multiple issues may share the same rank; 1 = most important.

Republicans, conservatives, and liberals. According to this survey, which was conducted by the Field Research Corporation, Democrats and Republicans differ as to which issues each thinks is the most important.

While public schools and healthcare costs appear at the top for both parties, there is significant disagreement regarding crime, illegal immigration, protecting the environment, and poverty. Republicans place crime and illegal immigration among the most important issues, second and fifth, respectively. However, Democrats place these issues near the bottom: eighteenth and twenty-third, respectively. On the other hand,

Democrats are very concerned with the environment and poverty: fourth and fifth. Republicans rank these issues twenty-fifth and twenty-sixth, respectively.

The results for ideology are similar. There is little disagreement between conservatives and liberals about the importance of public schools and healthcare costs. However, the two ideologies have significant differences on other issues: illegal drugs, illegal immigration, protecting the environment, and taxes. Conservatives think that illegal drugs and illegal immigration are equally as important as public schools, placing these issues in a three-way tie for first. However, illegal drugs and illegal immigration barely register on the liberal's radar screen, being ranked at twenty-sixth and twenty-eighth, respectively. Furthermore, conservatives think taxes are an important policy area—fifth— while the liberals do not—twenty-seventh. On the other hand, liberals show a high degree of concern about the environment, placing this issue in fourth place, while conservatives rank it twenty-sixth.

In table 3.2, we examine the same question from the perspectives of gender and age. With respect to gender, there is little difference between males and females over the importance of public schools and health care costs. This follows the same pattern as partisanship and ideology, variables for which there were no significant difference on these issues. However, significant differences appear on the following issues: poverty, traffic congestion, taxes, and illegal immigration. Females place a relatively high level of importance on poverty—seventh—while males place this issue strikingly low at twenty-fourth. On the other hand, males are concerned about taxes, traffic congestion, and illegal immigration— fourth, seventh, and ninth, respectively—while females are, for the most part, unconcerned with these issues—seventeenth, nineteenth, and twenty-fifth.

Analysis of the age variable reveals the importance of public schools and healthcare costs. However, significant differences appear in the areas of terrorism and security, higher education, unemployment, traffic congestion, and the state's economy. Higher education was a top concern for those age eighteen to thirty-nine and for those age forty to fifty-nine. Yet, higher education was not an important issue for those sixty and above. Conversely, in light of the 9/11 attacks, terrorism and security registered high with those 60 and above, yet, curiously, the two younger age brackets placed the issue much lower. As for those in the middle, the state's economy ranked high for those age forty to fifty-nine, yet those in the younger and older brackets placed the issue near the bottom.

Table 3.2.   Rank of Issue Importance by Gender and Age

Issue	Gender		Age		
	Male	Female	18–39	40–59	60+
Public Schools	2	1	1	2	3
Crime	13	5	11	5	14
Illegal Drugs	11	3	18	8	2
Healthcare Costs	1	2	3	1	1
Illegal Immigration	9	19	17	11	6
Electricity Costs	7	7	18	13	16
Taxes	4	17	15	7	9
Higher Education	4	5	2	8	22
Job Creation	10	10	11	8	9
Electricity Supply	7	7	18	13	16
State Economy	21	14	22	5	22
Terrorism and Security	19	14	16	20	3
State Budget Deficit	21	23	25	21	16
Public Health System	3	4	4	3	7
Cost of Living	4	10	4	13	9
Traffic Congestion	7	25	18	21	3
Gun Control	16	9	11	15	9
Housing Costs	16	18	6	19	22
Air and Water Pollution	13	10	9	17	9
Population Growth	20	23	21	24	5
Abortion	27	26	24	26	27
Water Supply	16	21	23	15	16
Welfare	25	22	27	25	20
Unemployment	23	14	8	23	19
Protecting Environment	11	13	7	11	22
Poverty	24	7	14	18	20
Race Relations	25	27	26	27	26
Government Services	28	27	28	28	28

Source: Field poll, February 2000 (Mark DeCamillo, director): <field.com/fieldpollonline/subscribers/COT-02-Feb-Issues.pdf> (accessed 4 May 2002).

Note: Ties are possible; multiple issues may share the same rank; 1 = most important.

MEDIA

The media are the primary means by which people receive political information. The media consist of television, radio, the printed press (newspapers, magazines, and newsletters), and the Internet. The media are not neutral, nor do they simply transmit information. They shape the nature of the information people receive, sometimes consciously and sometimes unconsciously.[13] However, media coverage of state and local politics is scarce. Most of the focus, even for the local press, is placed upon national politics.

For most of American history, the media were organs of a particular political party. There were Democratic newspapers and Republican newspapers. The editors of the so-called partisan press would shape stories to the advantage of their favorite candidates. As methods of communication and the American public became more sophisticated, it became more difficult for newspapers to characterize events in a certain manner. As telephones and radio allowed for quicker communication, people no longer had to wait for a newspaper to write, edit, and print a story. Political parties no longer felt the need to support newspapers as it became more difficult to shape public opinion through the partisan press.

To make up for this lost business, newspapers turned to sensationalism in the form of **muckraking** and **yellow journalism**. The media empire of William Randolph Hearst, headquartered in California, epitomized this change in journalism, and Hearst papers were the pioneers in these areas. Muckraking involves the exposure of corrupt practices in business and in government. Today, programs like *20/20* (ABC), *Dateline* (NBC), and *60 Minutes* (CBS) and Internet sites like *The Drudge Report* (www.-drudgereport.com) are heirs to the great muckraking tradition started by Hearst. Almost every local television news broadcast in California will include a muckraking story nightly. Furthermore, newspapers and radio stations routinely feature stories of government corruption and business malpractice.[14] Yellow journalism, on the other hand, often involves bald untruths or wild exaggerations. Yellow journalism is also known as tabloid journalism and is concerned with bizarre supernatural phenomena, celebrity gossip, or worldwide conspiracies.[15]

Over the past eighty years, with the rise of professional journalism schools, the media sought to recast itself as unbiased transmitters of information. The goal of modern journalism has been to present the news with as little editorializing as possible. However, it is doubtful that the media fulfills their goal. One need only examine the editorial pages of the following newspapers and the stories selected for publication in order to determine that the political opinion of reporters does influence the type of coverage that an issue or political leader receives: the *San Francisco Chronicle* (liberal), the *Los Angeles Times* (liberal), and the *Orange County Register* (conservative).

For the first half of the twentieth century, the dominant news medium was the newspaper. In the second half of the century, however, television took center stage, and network and local newscasts became the prime means of political communication. Now, as we enter a new century, newspapers and network television news are being challenged by the so-called **new media:** cable television, talk radio, and the Internet. The new media operate in a more segmented market, catering to narrow, well-defined areas of public opinion. Particular shows or websites are specifically geared to targeted audiences. The days of the general service radio or television station are over; in fact, it is quite possible that we might be entering a new era of the partisan press.

Entertainment Industry Influence

The influence of the entertainment industry on state politics is limited. Because the federal government has jurisdiction over the entertainment industry via the Federal Communications Commission, most of the entertainment industry's lobbying efforts focus on federal issues. Also, many Hollywood stars parlay their high visibility into elected office or positions of political influence. The late Sonny Bono became mayor of Palm Springs and was then elected to Congress. Actor and director Rob Reiner successfully led a drive to increase the tobacco tax in California through a statute initiative in 1998. Finally, California's media has a large impact on national news and opinion. California has three of the twenty largest newspapers in the United States and hosts many of the national news and entertainment programs that shape public opinion not only in California or the United States, but also worldwide.

CONCLUSION

With modern polling techniques, political leaders can maintain a daily watch over the ebbs and flows of opinion on a variety of issues. However, there is no such thing as *a* public opinion. Public opinion is divided into various segments: its major division is between the mass public and the elite public. The relative interest of the mass and elite publics determines the saliency of an issue. The less salient the issue, the more likely a political leader is to interject his or her private opinion on the matter. Public interest in a particular issue takes on the characteristic of what is known as an attention cycle, and it is a rare issue that maintains public interest throughout the entirety of this cycle. The most fundamental ideological division in public opinion is that between conservatives and liberals.

The media are the primary means by which people receive political information. Media consist of television, radio, the printed press (newspapers, magazines, and newsletters), and the Internet, and these all shape the nature of the information people receive. Television, the printed press, radio stations, and websites routinely feature stories of government corruption and business malpractice. California is home to three of the twenty largest newspapers in the United States and to many of the national news and entertainment programs that shape public opinion not only in California or the United States, but also worldwide.

NOTES

1. Alexis de Tocqueville, *Democracy in America*, trans., ed., and with an introduction by Harvey C. Mansfield and Delba Winthrop (Chicago: The University of Chicago Press, 2000), 243.

2. Tocqueville, *Democracy in America*, 177.

3. Joseph M. Bessette, *The Mild Voice of Reason* (Chicago: University of Chicago Press, 1994), 35.

4. For an outstanding account of face-to-face interaction between political leaders and their constituents, see Richard F. Fenno, Jr., *Homestyle* (Boston: Little, Brown, 1978).

5. John W. Kingdon, *Congressmen's Voting Decisions,* 3rd ed. (Ann Arbor: University of Michigan Press, 1989).

6. Anthony Downs, "Up and Down with Ecology: The 'Issue Attention Cycle,'" *The Public Interest* 28 (Summer 1972): 38–50.

7. Sharon Bernstein and Robert A. Rosenblatt, "Average HMO Medicare Rate Set to Double," *Los Angeles Times* (16 September 2000): 1.

8. Susan Warner, "Drug Firms Get a Dose of Disdain in this Election Year," *San Diego Union-Tribune* (2 September 2000): C1.

9. *The Federalist,* 288–293.

10. Today, ideology is synonymous with political prejudice, and its connotation is that all political opinions are equally groundless. Since, in the modern mind, there are no natural standards, the expression of opinion is merely the expression of will. While we are forced to use the term "ideology" because of its ubiquitous quality, we mean something more like political opinion as opposed to political will. For a reasonably accessible discussion of this, see Leo Strauss and Joseph Cropsey, "Introduction," in *History of Political Philosophy,* 3rd ed. (Chicago: University of Chicago Press, 1987), 1–6.

11. It is a matter of debate just what it is that conservatives defend. A misunderstanding of the nature of the thing to be defended could have profound and lasting effects. See Harry V. Jaffa, *American Conservatism and the American Founding* (Durham, N.C.: Carolina Academic Press, 1984).

12. Louise G. White, *Political Analysis* (Pacific Grove, Calif.: Brooks/Cole, 1990).

13. Josh Getlin, "Regarding the Media; for Whom the Polls Toll—the Candidate Who's Trailing," *Los Angeles Times* (18 September 2000): E1.

14. An example would be the Rampart scandal in the Los Angeles Police Department. See Shawn Hubler, "Truth and Consequences for the LAPD," *Los Angeles Times* (18 September 2000): B1.

15. Michael Taylor, "The Reign of S.F.'s Monarch of the Dailies; Hearst Media Empire Started with Examiner," *San Francisco Chronicle* (7 August 1999): A9.

Chapter Four

Parties and Interest Groups

After the freedom to act alone, the most natural to man is that of combining his efforts with the efforts of those like him and acting in common. The right of association appears to me to be almost as inalienable in its nature as individual freedom.[1]

Political parties and interest groups are formed by citizens who share certain opinions about government. Political parties produce candidates for public office. The association of a candidate with one party or the other—Democrat or Republican, for example—is emblematic of the candidate's opinions about government. In the best sense, political parties are the standard bearers of the principles of the American Revolution. The dominance of a particular political party over a period of time depends upon its ability to restore the people's confidence in republican government.[2]

Interest groups are associations of like-minded people who attempt to influence government officials to support or oppose certain policies. Interest groups are narrower in scope than parties are; they are organized by people with specific economic or social concerns. Organizations such as a chamber of commerce, a business group, and a labor union are examples of economic interest groups. On the other hand, the National Rifle Association, an organization dedicated to protecting a person's right to own firearms, and the Million Mom March, an organization that is opposed to such rights, are examples of social interest groups.[3]

Within the confines of state politics, there is an inverse relationship between the strength of political parties and interest groups.[4] If political parties are strong in a state, interest groups tend to be weak. If interest groups are strong, parties will be weak. The latter condition describes the nature of democracy in California.

CALIFORNIA POLITICAL PARTIES

Official Definitions

Political parties, which are regulated by the State of California,[5] are recognized and allowed to nominate candidates for state offices if they can meet at least one of two requirements. The first is by means of registration: a political party will be officially recognized if the number of Californians registered in that party is equal to or greater than 1 percent of the total number of voters in the most recent gubernatorial election.[6] For example, the total number of voters in the 1998 gubernatorial election was 8,617,649. In order to qualify for the 2002 election by means of registration, a political party must have had at least 86,177 registered voters.

The second method of qualification is by means of petition. If the number of signatures on a petition is equal to or greater than 10 percent of the voters in the last general election, then the political party is considered official. Using the 1998 general election figures, a successful party petition would require 861,765 signatures. In 2002, the officially recognized political parties in California were the American Independent, Democratic, Green, Libertarian, Natural Law, Republican, and Reform parties. However, the Democratic and Republican parties are the two dominant parties, and the remaining parties share only a fraction of the remaining registered voters.

Why Only Two Major Parties?

The Democratic and Republican parties are the two major political parties in California and in the rest of the nation. The main reason for this is the nature of our election system. Other nations, like Israel and Germany, have more than two major political parties because they employ an election system called **proportional representation (PR)**. For example, in a PR legislative election, the number of seats a party controls is determined by the percent of the vote it receives in the election. If a party receives 10 percent of the vote, it will receive 10 percent of the seats in the legislature. If it receives 60 percent of the vote, it will receive 60 percent of the seats. Because it is possible to win seats in the legislature with only a small percent of the vote, candidates have an incentive to split off and form a variety of parties.

The United States, for the most part, employs a system of **single member districts (SMD)**. For example, in the California Legislature, representatives come from eighty districts in the assembly and forty in the senate (this will be discussed more in chapter 6 on the legislature). In order to have one of its candidates win a seat in these elections; a political party's candidate must win a **plurality** of votes—the most votes out of all the other candidates running for office, but not necessarily the majority—in a specific district. Under this system, candidates of a particular party could consistently receive 10 percent of the vote, but *never* gain any seats in a legislature. Therefore, a candidate does not have a great incentive to be associated with a minor party. Given the mathematical reality of the plurality requirement, it is natural that a two-party system would develop.

The more pressing question regarding the two-party system is not the explanation for its existence but whether or not it is just. On one side of the question, it could be said that the SMD system limits the choices of voters. Instead of being able to cast a vote for a wide variety of parties, a voter is limited, in effect, to a choice between only two candidates. This limitation could be seen as undemocratic. On the other side of the argument is the belief that a two-party system increases the stability of a regime, with stability as one of the prime requirements for a successful republic. The SMD system forces fringe elements to join one of the two major parties in order to have an effective political voice. Thus, the political system is more moderate and less likely to produce strong fascist or communist parties. When one compares the politics of PR nations with those of SMD nations, the truth of the preceding statement is evident.

However, the concerns of those who are wary of the political ossification that can occur with a two-party system are justified. When the two major parties fail to understand and deal with the pressing crises of the day, the health of the regime is in jeopardy. In such situations, the fate of the country might depend upon the rise of a **third party,** but because of the SMD system, three parties cannot coexist for any length of time. In order to survive, the upstart party must become one of the two major parties while one of the existing major parties must fade away.

This very phenomenon occurred once before in American history. During the 1830s and the 1840s, the two major political parties in the United States were the Democrats and the Whigs. By the 1850s, the failure of each adequately to address the question of slavery led to the rise of a new party. The rise of this new party caused the Whig Party to disappear, and this new party replaced the Democratic Party as the dominant American political party for the next seventy years. This upstart political party was the Republican Party.

Party Structure

Each of the political parties in California has the same basic structure. The most basic level of organization is the county central committee, for which voters directly elect members. The next level of organization is the state central committee, and its members are selected in a variety of ways: from the county committees, from party candidates for office, and from representatives from various clubs or organizations associated with each party. In addition to these organizations, there is a state chair for each political party who is elected by the state committee of each party.

Other important members of California political parties include each party's delegates to the national conventions and each party's representatives for the national party committees. Official party organizations, on the whole, are less powerful than they were a century ago because the party has very little control over the selection of candidates and, therefore, the policy proposals that those candidates espouse. Today, the most important leaders of a party are the officeholders affiliated with it.

Weakened Parties

Political parties in the United States are, for the most part, weak. A condition of weakness is defined by a party's inability to affect which candidates will hold office, the policies they propose once in office, and the selection of those who serve in the government bureaucracy. This weakness is the legacy of the Progressive movement, which was a major political force from the 1880s to the 1920s. Prior to this time, political party organizations could control which candidates would represent their party in the general elections. If a candidate won the general election and failed to follow the policy opinions of party leaders, they could be removed from the party's slot in the next general election. Therefore, officeholders would be wise to accommodate the leaders of their party organizations if they wanted to maintain their positions. In addition, elected officials—especially mayors and governors—had the responsibility for directly hiring people to fill government positions. A mayor, governor, or other elected official wanting to maintain good standing with a party would be sure to hire government employees who had been approved by the party organization.

Today, almost none of this occurs. Political party organizations cannot select nominees in a general election, for that selection is left to the voters in primary elections. Furthermore, elected officials have almost no control over government employment. While they are allowed to hire a few close associates as advisors, over 90 percent of government employees are hired by means of the civil service system, whereby government jobs are given to people on the basis of merit rather than by party affiliation. Thus, the party organization has very little control over substantive government actions. In addition, local and judicial elections in California are nonpartisan; candidates are not allowed to advertise their party affiliation on the ballot.

The particular weakness of California parties can be traced to Governor Hiram Johnson (1911–1917). As detailed earlier in the text, Johnson was elected on a platform of eliminating the corrupt practices of political machines. He believed that corruption, and therefore bad government, would be eliminated by bringing the process into the open by means of a civil service and primary elections.

Governor Johnson sought to eliminate political parties as election institutions by the employment of a system known as **cross-filing.** Candidates for office could qualify as a nominee for either or *both* political parties, and political parties were prohibited from endorsing candidates in their own primary. If a candidate could win the nomination of both political parties, which often happened, the general election would be a *fait accompli.* There is no weaker condition for a political party to be in than to be unable to prevent members of the opposite party from representing it in the general election. Although cross-filing ended in 1959, the party structure in California has never fully recovered.[7]

Why, then, do we pay any attention to California political parties? The answer is that while the organization of the party is weak, the identification by candidates with one party or the other is still meaningful. Democratic candidates tend to take different positions on issues than Republican candidates do, and they also tend to act on those different policy opinions once they are in office.[8] Examples of major issues upon which the two parties significantly disagree are: conservation, crime, gun rights, homosexuality, school choice, and taxation. Democrats are more inclined toward stringent environmental regulation, less likely to favor tough anticrime measures, opposed to gun rights, in favor of increased acceptance of homosexuality, against school choice, and generally opposed to tax cuts. Republicans are generally the opposite.

Relative Strength of the Two Parties

The Democratic Party has been the strongest political party in California since the 1950s. Democrats have had a clear advantage in terms of the percent of registered voters, which explains their relative dominance in the assembly and senate. From 1954 to 1998, the Republicans won control of the senate in only two elections and won the assembly in only four elections.

However, the scope of Democratic dominance declined after 1982. Amidst the national influence of Ronald Reagan during the 1980s, Republican registration increased substantially as Democratic registration dipped to below 50 percent. This partially accounts for a string of Republican victories in gubernatorial elections. However, the election of Gray Davis in 1998 brought this Republican gubernatorial winning streak to an end, two years after the GOP had lost control of the state legislature. Unlike the Republican rise in the 1980s, Davis's victory was not accompanied by a rise in Democratic registration. In fact, Davis's victory came as both Democratic registration and Republican registration were declining. Governor Davis has made a point to attempt to distance himself from both the Republicans and from the Democrat-controlled legislature in a bid to win support from independents. This rise of the nonaffiliated voter is more evidence of the weak state of political parties in California.[9]

INTEREST GROUPS

Interest groups are associations of likeminded people who attempt to influence government officials to support or oppose certain policies. The nature and activity of interest groups has been a matter of debate since the founding of our nation.[10] Some argue that interest groups are merely the tools of the elite, while others argue that interest groups are the means by which all segments of society make their opinions known to officeholders.[11] In fact, it is quite possible that interest groups emerge as certain elements of society become dominant, counterbalancing this larger force in order to create equilibrium.[12] However, it is also just as possible that people join interest groups to get material benefits—such as health plans, discounts, and magazines—or are automatically affiliated with an interest group simply because they are employed in a certain profession, such as those involved with labor unions, trade groups, and professional associations.[13]

Regulation of Interest Groups

Interest groups in California are not ad hoc organizations that gather from time to time when the need arises. In order to contact officeholders and attempt to influence policy, they must register with the State of California. This has been a requirement since 1893, when laws were passed to limit the political influence of the Southern Pacific Railroad, which at that time was the state's most powerful interest group. Interest groups must also file periodic statements concerning their expenses and campaign finance activities. California passed even more stringent regulations in 1949, in response to the controversial activities of Artie Samish, a powerful Sacramento lobbyist. The most recent major piece of legislation to limit the activities of interest groups was the Political Reform Act of 1974. Under this act, the Political Reform Division was created and placed under the authority of the secretary of state.[14]

Interest Group Activities

There are three main interest group activities: *direct lobbying, grassroots activity,* and *campaign finance.* Direct lobbying involves direct contact between an agent of an interest group and an officeholder, usually a legislator. They are called lobbyists because it has been the tradition that interest group members attempt to speak with legislators in the lobby of the legislature as they are coming to or going from a floor session. A lobbyist is usually hired by an interest group to communicate with officeholders and express the concerns that members of an interest group might have with a particular bill. Most often, a lobbyist attempts to influence a legislator by supplying information that can prove quite useful to a legislator. California legislators must consider hundreds of bills in a two-year legislative period, and it is difficult to make decisions as to which to support and which to oppose. A lobbyist who gains a reputation for supplying a legislator with good information can be a real asset to a legislator as well as to his or her respective group.

One example of a successful lobbyist is the energetic Don Novey, the president of the California Correctional Peace Officers Association (CCPOA). With thousands of members, the CCPOA is one of the more influential lobbying groups in Sacramento. In fact, its influence is so strong that other groups, most notably those representing Indian gaming interests, have forged alliances with the CCPOA to strengthen their lobbying positions.[15]

Grassroots activity defines any actions by large groups of people, and can range from phone calls to protest marches. Unlike lobbying, which involves carefully hired representatives, grassroots activity is the arena of the masses. However, this does not mean that it is less effective; in fact, it can be more powerful than lobbying. A well-timed avalanche of

calls, e-mails, faxes, and letters to a legislator's office can have an instan-
taneous effect on whether or not a legislator will support or oppose a
bill. What the mass of citizens may lack in expertise, they more than
compensate for in sheer numbers.[16] Furthermore, grassroots activity is
often initiated by organizations with professional full-time staff who can
advise citizens in how to take effective action.

The final category of interest group activity is campaign finance. Interest groups make donations to various candidates. Some donate to
officeholders, hoping to influence their vote. Others donate to officeholders as a reward for past votes. Recent research, however, demon-
strates that interest groups tend to give money to officeholders who
already agree with them.[17] In this way, campaign finance is one more
way that people help their allies and attempt to defeat their enemies.

Relative Activities

One should not conclude that one issue is more important than another
because its interest groups spend more than other issues' interest groups
do. Quite often, a large amount of spending means that during a particular legislative session, a specific category was more controversial than
others. No one would seriously argue that agriculture is unimportant in
California politics, but its interest groups have relatively minor
expenses. This could be an indication that, compared with other issues,
agriculture is not as controversial in state government circles.

Lobbyists representing other governments—cities, counties, etc.—
were the top spenders according to the most recent reports available.[18]
Government lobbyists spent $52.9 million in the last election cycle. Lob-
byists for the health industry came in second place with $41.5 million in
expenditures. Manufacturing and industrial groups were third with
$34.6 million while finance and insurance groups came in fourth with
$29.7 million. Rounding out the top five were education groups with
$27.5 million spent to influence policymakers.

However, when disaggregated into individual expenditures by specific
organizations, a slightly different picture emerges.[19] The California
Teachers Association is the most active single lobbying organization
with $5.7 million in expenditures. Pacific Telesis came in a close second
with $5.1 million. The Western States Petroleum Association was third
with $3.9 million. The California Chamber of Commerce was not far
behind with $3.6 million and the beleaguered Edison International, in
the midst of the power crisis, spent $3.1 to present its case to those in
government.

Interest Groups as Factions

In *The Federalist* (no. 10), James Madison argued that one of the strengths of the new continental American republic, as opposed to the classical *polis,* would be in its having many factions as opposed to a few. Madison argued that the existence of only two or three factions within a small territory would lead to the creation of a majority faction, which would use its power to tyrannize over the minority factions. In America, with its size and scope, there is less of a chance that a majority faction would develop. No single interest is so large that it can act alone without cooperation from others. Therefore, interests are forced to compromise with one another.

The same could be said of California. The health industry is not so large that it could not be defeated by a coordinated effort of the manufacturing and finance interests. However, one must not take away from Madison's discussion the idea that it is the competition alone that guarantees the survival of the republic. Madison was not a social Darwinist; one need only read, *The Federalist* (no. 14), where Madison connects the discussion of a large republic with the moral purpose it was intended to achieve. Madison advocated a commercial republic of many "factions," so that an otherwise decent nation such as the United States would have the best chance to survive. There is nothing in Madison to make us believe that he would not have wished the same for the State of California.[20]

CONCLUSION

Political parties and interest groups are formed by citizens who share certain opinions about the nature of government. Political parties produce candidates for election to public office. Members of political parties tend to share a broad set of ideas concerning the nature of government. If political parties are strong in a state, interest groups will be weak; if interest groups are strong, parties will be weak. The Democratic and Republican parties are the two major political parties in California. California has two major political parties because, like the rest of the nation, it employs an SMD election system. Despite political party weakness in California, the identification of a candidate with one party or the other conveys important information to the voter.

Interest groups, which are narrower in scope than political parties, are associations of like-minded people who attempt to influence government officials to support or oppose certain policies. There are three main categories of interest group activity: *direct lobbying, grassroots activity,* and *campaign finance.* The five most active categories of interest groups are: government, health, manufacturing and industry, finance, and education.

NOTES

1. Alexis de Tocqueville, *Democracy in America*, trans., ed., and with an introduction by Harvey C. Mansfield and Delba Winthrop (Chicago: The University of Chicago Press, 2000), 185.

2. See Harry V. Jaffa, "The Nature and Origin of the American Party System," in *Equality and Liberty* (New York: Oxford University Press, 1965), 3–41. However, this is true only so long as the principles of the American Revolution are the animating principles of the regime.

3. Kathleen Les, "Business's Big Guns," in *California Government and Politics Annual 1998–1999* (Sacramento: StateNet, 1999), 43–44; Kathleen Les, "Labor Toils Mightily for a Select Few," *California Journal* 31 (May 2000): 46–49; and Cynthia H. Craft, "The Economic Silver Lining to Gun Laws," *California Journal* 31 (March 2000): 18–22.

4. The rise in strength of interest groups has coincided with the decline of parties. See evidence of this in Norman Ornstein, Thomas Mann, and Michael Malbin, *Vital Statistics on Congress, 1993–1994* (Washington, D.C., 1994). Further confirmation of this trend can be found in L. Harmon Zigler and Hendrik van Dalen, "Interest Groups in the States," in *Politics in the American States,* 2nd ed., eds. Herbert Jacob and Kenneth N. Vines (Boston: Little, Brown, 1974), 122–160.

5. Elections for local offices, judicial positions, and the Superintendent of Public Instruction are nonpartisan.

6. When a citizen registers to vote in California, he or she is given the option of declaring a political party preference. A voter registers for a political party when they identify themselves with such a party on their voter registration form.

7. Robert DiClerico, *Political Parties, Campaigns and Elections* (Upper Saddle River, N.J.: Prentice-Hall, 2000).

8. See selections from John G. Geer, ed., *Politicians and Party Politics* (Baltimore: Johns Hopkins University Press, 2000).

9. In addition to this account, one might consider the effects of divided government in California. Because of the initiative/referendum/recall process and the super-majority budget vote requirement, it is likely that the effects of divided government are even less pronounced in California. For a further discussion, see David Mayhew, *Divided We Govern* (New Haven: Yale University Press, 1991); Morris Fiorina, *Divided Government,* 2nd ed. (New York: Allyn and Bacon, 1996); and Peter F. Galderisi, ed., *Divided Government: Change, Uncertainty, and the Constitutional Order* (Lanham, Md.: Rowman & Littlefield, 1996).

10. *The Federalist,* 45–52.

11. E. E. Schattschneider, *The Semi-Sovereign People* (New York: Holt, Rinehart, and Winston, 1960).

12. David B. Truman, *The Governmental Process: Political Interests and Public Opinion* (New York: Knopf, 1951).

13. Mancur Olson, Jr., *The Logic of Collective Action* (New York: Schocken, 1968); and Jack Walker, *Mobilizing Interest Groups in America* (Ann Arbor: University of Michigan Press, 1991).

14. The Political Reform Division has the following official responsibilities: regulate state and local campaign committees that raise funds for non-federal elections; receive and verify campaign disclosure statements; regulate campaign documents; provide public access to all campaign information; and impose fines and penalties for failure to comply with regulations.

15. Noel Brinkerhoff, "The Strangest of Bedfellows," *California Journal* 31 (May 2000): 24–28, 31.

16. Conservative and business groups have been more effective in grassroots activity as of late. See Bill Ainsworth, "Astroturf Lobbying," *California Government and Politics Annual: 1998–1999* (Sacramento: StateNet), 39–40.

17. Carol S. Weissert and William S. Weissert, *Governing Health: The Politics of Health Policy* (Baltimore: Johns Hopkins University Press, 1996).

18. State of California: <www.ss.ca.gov/prd/lobreport00_8qtr/chart1.htm> (accessed 4 May 2002).

19. State of California: <www.ss.ca.gov/prd/lobreport00_8qtr/chart4.htm> (accessed 4 May 2002).

20. *The Federalist*, no. 14.

Chapter Five

Campaigns and Elections

If passing events sometimes succeed in combating the passions of democracy, enlightenment, and above all mores, exert a no less powerful, and more lasting, influence on its penchants.[1]

Elections are the vital link between the citizen and the government in a republic, and state and local elections afford a citizen the chance to decide matters that are closest to home. This link can be direct or indirect. In *representative democracy,* citizens may vote for people they trust to make decisions on whether or not to support certain issues. In *direct democracy,* citizens have the opportunity to vote on issues themselves, without any mediation from representatives.

The American founders were wary of direct democracy and for good reason.[2] Until the time of the American founding, human experiments with democracy had been a disaster. Every democracy that had come into existence had degenerated into anarchy or tyranny, and almost all of these had been direct democracies. The founders rescued the reputation of democracy by creating representative institutions in which people could place trusted agents in office to act on their behalf. These agents would gather together in an environment of deliberation and debate to carry out these actions.

While a representative democracy is not a guarantee that wise decisions would emerge, the founders thought that it would give the reason of the public the best chance to emerge. The prevalence of direct democracy at the state level of government, and particularly in California, poses significant questions about the understanding of democracy bequeathed to us by the founders. Can a system of direct democracy coexist with a representative democracy and provide a result that enables us to maintain "life, liberty, and the pursuit of happiness"?[3]

ALL ELECTIONS ARE STATE ELECTIONS

The legacy of American *federalism* is that, in a sense, all elections are state elections. Elections for the presidency, Congress, governorship, state legislature, state judiciary, and local offices are conducted by the states. A federal system is one in which sovereignty is shared between the national and state governments. For example, we do not elect a president by popular vote in a single national election.[4] Presidents are elected by means of the Electoral College, by which a separate election occurs within each state.[5] Furthermore, members of Congress—senators and representatives—are elected as residents of a particular state, not as national citizens. The focus of this chapter will be on elections for officers who will preside over California government: the governor, elected executives, legislators, judges, and local officials.

Three basic election issues are California's voter qualifications, use of absentee ballots, and candidate qualifications.

Voter Qualifications

The chief elections officer in California is the secretary of state, who is responsible for the enforcement of candidate eligibility requirements, maintenance of registration rolls, distribution of ballots, and the overall integrity of California elections. The secretary of state is assisted at the local level by county clerks or county registrars of voters.

A person is eligible to vote in an election if he or she has reached eighteen years of age by election day and is a United States citizen, an official resident of the state of California, and not a felon serving a sentence in prison or on parole. In addition, a person must register to vote at least twenty-nine days before an election.

Absentee Ballots

Absentee ballots are supplied to any California voter upon request, and a voter who has requested an absentee ballot will receive one in the mail. The voter completes this ballot and mails it to the appropriate county official. These ballots are not opened or counted until election day. The original idea behind absentee ballots was to provide an opportunity to vote for those who would be *absent* from the jurisdiction at the time of the election, but others can use absentee ballots as well.

Candidate Qualifications

A person's eligibility as a candidate for office depends upon the office being sought. There are different requirements for the elected executives, which include the offices of governor, lieutenant governor, secretary of state, and attorney general, treasurer, controller, superintendent of public instruction, insurance commissioner, and the members of the Board of Equalization. To be eligible for these offices, a candidate must be at least eighteen years of age, a United States citizen for at least five years, and a California resident for at least five years. For all other state and local offices—such as legislator, judge, mayor, or member of a local school board—a person must simply be at least eighteen years of age, a United States citizen, and a current resident of the state of California.

TYPES OF ELECTIONS

Elections occur in California several times a year. State and local elections each have their own schedule. Elections for governor and the other directly elected executives occur every four years and take place in even-numbered, nonpresidential years (e.g., 1998, 2002, and 2006). State assembly members have two-year terms and stand for reelection in even-numbered years. Senators have four-year terms, with only half of the senate up for reelection every two years: those from even-numbered districts stand for election in the same years in which the governor is up for election, and those from odd-numbered districts stand for election in presidential election years. Judicial elections have their own special characteristics. The years in which elections for local offices take place vary with each locality, and many local elections take place in odd-numbered years.

Partisan and Nonpartisan Elections

Candidates for most elected executive offices and for the legislature compete in **partisan elections,** in which candidates for these offices may run as representatives of political parties. Political party identification conveys to the voter a general impression of the opinions and potential actions of the candidates. Democratic candidates generally have different views about the proper role of government than Republican candidates do. Candidates for the superintendent of public instruction, the state judiciary, and all local offices run in **nonpartisan** elections, in which candidates do not run as official representatives of a particular party.

The idea behind nonpartisan elections is that certain functions of government—education, the law, and local matters—are not appropriate subjects of partisan debate. However, what is partisanship but the organization of people around particular ideas about the appropriate role of government, including education, the law, and local matters? Elected officials in nonpartisan offices cannot leave their opinions about these matters at the office door. The conduct of their job requires specific opinions and solutions for certain problems.

Primary Elections

For most of the nineteenth century, the central committee of each state's political parties selected candidates for office. Such a system was known as a *political machine*. Since the beginning of the twentieth century, however, the predominant method of selecting candidates for general elections has been the primary election.

Whether partisan or nonpartisan, there are two main types of elections for offices in California: **primary elections** and **general elections.** A partisan primary election is used to determine which candidates will represent each party in the general election, and a nonpartisan primary is used to winnow the field down to an eventual office holder. The winner of a general election attains the office under consideration.

In a typical nonpartisan primary—a city council seat, for example—there will be several candidates who seek to hold the office. If any candidate receives a majority of the vote, then that candidate is awarded the office. If, however, no candidate receives a majority, the general election will take place between the two candidates receiving the most votes in the primary.

A partisan primary is different. In most of these primary elections, several candidates from each party face off against one another for the privilege of representing their party in the general election for that office. The people with the most votes from each party will face one another in the general election. However, it is often the case that an **incumbent**—a person who already holds the office and is running for reelection—will not face any primary challengers and will automatically move on to the general election. Political parties generally discourage primary challenges to incumbent candidates for fear that a strong primary challenge will leave the candidate with less money and energy for the general election campaign, a race in which they could lose the office to the other party.

Types of Partisan Primaries

There have been four main types of primaries employed in the United States: closed, open, runoff, and blanket. Each state has the responsibility to determine which method will be used. A *closed primary* is one in which only registered members of a particular party may vote; only registered Democrats are allowed to select Democratic candidates, only registered Republicans are allowed to select Republican candidates, and so forth. An *open primary* is one in which voters may participate in a party's primary without having to register with the party. A *runoff primary,* which is less common and is limited primarily to the South, is similar to a nonpartisan primary. All candidates, whether Republican or Democrat, appear on the same ballot. If any candidate receives a majority of the vote, they are awarded the office. If no candidate achieves a majority, then the top two candidates from the primary election face off in the general election. In a runoff primary, it is quite possible that the two candidates in the general election could be from the same party.

This brings us to the final method of primary election, known as a *blanket primary.* The blanket primary was used in California from 1998 to 2000 before being declared unconstitutional by the United States Supreme Court.[6] It is a hybrid of the open and runoff primaries. A voter can participate in a blanket primary without having to register for any party. In a blanket primary, all of the candidates for a particular office—whether they are Republicans, Democrats, Libertarians, or Green—appear on the same ballot. A voter may decide to select a Republican candidate for governor, a Democratic candidate for lieutenant governor, a Libertarian for attorney general, and so on. After the votes are counted, the top candidates from each party square off in the general election.

This method of primary is quite controversial[7] because it is quite possible that members of one party might try to influence a general election by participating in the other party's primary and selecting what, in their opinion, would be the weaker candidate. Whether or not these strategies have been employed successfully is a matter of debate. However, it is clear that if the blanket primary were allowed to continue, it would have placed political parties, already weakened by civil service reform and the primary system, in an even weaker position.

Currently, California has a modified closed primary system. Registered party members may only vote in their own party's primary. However, at the discretion of each political party, nonaffiliated voters may participate in the primary election of any political party. As of the 2002

election cycle, both the Democratic and Republican parties allow nonaffiliated voters to participate in their respective primaries.

Primary elections for statewide offices take place on the first Tuesday
after the first Monday in March of the election year. General elections
for statewide office take place on the first Tuesday after the first Monday
in November of the same election year. The dates of local primary and
general elections vary by locality. Finally, special elections can occur at
various times of the year due to unexpected vacancies caused by resigna-
tion or death.

DIRECT DEMOCRACY

There are three types of mechanisms by which voters can have the final
say on a matter of policy: initiatives, referenda, and recall attempts, all
of which can be placed on either a primary or a general election ballot.[8]
Whether or not a measure is placed on a primary or general election
ballot, it is decided within that single election. Initiatives are employed
in twenty-one states, and there is no primary for competing initiatives.
Referenda are employed in all states except Alabama, and recall elections are available to residents in sixteen states.[9]

The Initiative

Initiatives got their name because they are policy proposals that are initiated by individuals or groups, not by the state legislature. There are two
types of initiatives: statute and constitutional. Voters decide whether a
statute initiative may become part of the California Code, and whether
a constitution initiative may become part of the California Constitution.
In order to place a statute initiative on the ballot, supporters must collect
petition signatures equivalent to or greater than 5 percent of the total
votes cast in the most recent gubernatorial election. The signature
requirement for a constitution initiative is 8 percent. If either initiative
is placed on the ballot, it needs a majority vote to be approved.

The Referendum

On a referendum proposal, voters are asked to judge an action previously taken by the state legislature. There are three main types of referenda: statute, constitutional, and mandatory. A statute referendum is
proposed when an individual or group wishes to remove an element

from the California Code that was enacted by the legislature. The qualifying procedure is identical to that for a statute initiative, and if a majority of voters approves the referendum, the statute is removed from the California Code.

The remaining two types of referenda are placed on the ballot by the legislature. A constitutional referendum is placed on the ballot by a two-thirds vote of each chamber—twenty-seven in the senate, fifty-four in the assembly—with each chamber voting separately. If a majority of voters approve the measure, it becomes part of the California Constitution. A mandatory referendum is also placed on the ballot after a two-thirds vote from each chamber. Mandatory referenda involve the approval of government bonds, which are used to fund large construction projects or other significant capital outlays. These referenda are called "mandatory" because the legislature and the governor cannot issue bonds that are backed by taxpayer dollars unless the measure is approved by the voters. However, urgency measures (which are discussed in chapter 6, on the legislature) are exempt from the referendum process.

The Recall

State and local officers can be removed before the expiration of their term by means of a recall petition and election. In order for a recall election to take place, supporters must obtain a minimum number of signatures, and the amount required to force an election varies with the office. For directly elected executives, except for the four district representatives on the state Board of Equalization, the number of signatures must be at least 12 percent of the total votes cast in the most recent election for that office, with the further stipulation that the signatures must be collected from at least five counties. For state legislators, members of the Board of Equalization, and appellate court judges, the signatures must equal at least 20 percent of the total votes cast in the last election for that office. For local officials, the number of signatures required varies with the size of the locality:

- 30 percent if the voter registration is less than 1,000,
- 25 percent if the registration is less than 10,000 but at least 1,000,
- 20 percent if the registration is less than 50,000 but at least 10,000,
- 15 percent if the registration is less than 100,000 but at least 50,000,
- 10 percent if the registration is 100,000 or above.[10]

If enough signatures are collected, two separate questions are placed on the ballot. The first is whether or not the officer should be recalled.

The second asks for a replacement officeholder should a majority of those voting choose to recall the sitting officeholder. If a majority decides to recall the officer, the person receiving the most votes on the second question takes office. Recall elections are rare and are more common for local officials than for state officials. However, such actions need not be frequent to be memorable, and their impact can be profound and last for decades. The memory of just one such election removing a colleague can lead a legislator to abandon any notions of drifting too far from the sentiments of the constituents.

Memorable Initiatives

Californians face a barrage of proposals in the form of initiatives and referenda, and a typical ballot contains a dozen or so proposals.[11] Very often, the initiative or referendum process is used by governors, legislators, and interest groups to obtain desired policy goals after failing to enact them in the normal legislative process. In fact, a huge commercial enterprise has developed around direct democracy in California. Petition gathering, polling, legal counseling, and campaign consulting amount to a major industry in the Golden State. The situation is so complex that sometimes a group or official opposed to a policy idea successfully places an initiative on the ballot, hoping for it to be defeated!

Even though the system is complex, direct democracy remains popular with the people of California.[12] Some of the more memorable initiatives that have passed concerned property tax relief (Proposition 13, 1978), term limits (Proposition 140, 1990), illegal immigration (Proposition 187, 1994), the scaling back of affirmative action (Proposition 209, 1996), the scaling back of bilingual education (Proposition 227, 1998), approving casino gambling (Proposition 5, 1998), increased tobacco taxes (Proposition 10, 1998), and the protection of marriage (Proposition 22, 2000). Unless the initiative is drafted otherwise, most are required to go into effect immediately upon passage—unless, of course, the proposal is struck down in the courts.

The Role of the Courts

Even if the voters approve an initiative, it may still be invalidated in a federal or state court. Most of the time, it is the federal courts that act to strike down California initiatives. One reason for this could be the fact that state judges must stand for voter approval, while federal judges have lifetime appointments and thus have less to lose by making unpopular decisions.

A prominent example of judicial interference occurred with Proposition 187, which was approved by voters in 1994. Proposition 187, which was backed strongly by Governor Pete Wilson (1991–1999), sought to eliminate the state's financial responsibility for providing healthcare and education to illegal immigrants. This measure was invalidated with an immediate injunction in federal court and was never implemented. In the minds of many, the court system acts as an additional check on the direct democracy system, much like the checks and balances in the legislative process between the senate, assembly, and governor. However, there is some doubt as to whether or not this "judicial check" is in line with what the founders had intended for American democracy. The checks and balances of the federal system were designed to promote rational deliberation so that the reasoned judgment of the public would emerge.[13]

VITAL ELECTION STATISTICS

Campaign Finance

California elections are expensive. In the 1998 gubernatorial election, the two major candidates—Gray Davis and Dan Lungren—spent a total of $52,487,133. In 1976, when Jerry Brown defeated Evelle Younger, the total was only $5,709,806.[14] This is a dramatic increase, even when inflation is considered.[15] What is to be done about this? Some would argue that states must impose a spending cap, and that these expensive races limit the ability of the non-elite to participate in the system. According to this belief, campaign money is property and can be regulated by the government.

However, there is another side of this argument. Instead of being viewed as property, campaign money can be viewed a form of speech; as such, it is protected by both the California and United States Constitutions. If limits are placed on how much money a candidate can spend in an election, then those limits can, in effect, harm the ability of a candidate to present their message to voters and thus limit the candidate's right to free speech.[16] Furthermore, spending limits would favor incumbents, who already have an advantage in name recognition and media exposure,[17] and place a burden on challengers. In order to overcome the power of incumbents, challengers must often spend more than the incumbent. However, the successful implementation of term limits in California has made elections more accessible to challengers.[18]

Voter Turnout

Voter turnout can be measured in two ways: One method is to calculate the number of voters as a percent of the voting-age population. Out of all the people who were eligible to vote, which voters actually showed up at the polls? Another method is to calculate the number of voters as a percent of those registered. Historically, there is a significant difference between the two figures. Voter turnout as a percent of registered voters has consistently been above the 70 percent mark, while turnout as a percent of the population has been at or below 50 percent since 1970. Why the difference? It takes time to register and registration must take place at least twenty-nine days before the election. One cannot simply show up at the polls the day of the election and vote. Finally, turnout is much greater in state elections that coincide with a presidential election because people are more likely to vote during larger elections.

It is a matter of debate as to whether we should be concerned about declining levels of voter turnout. In one sense, the answer is yes because declining levels of participation reveal indifference toward the controversies of public life. Perhaps people are more distracted by the many forms of entertainment available to them or are cynical about government.[19] Declining turnout has led to a variety of campaigns to reverse this trend. However, one would assume that people would do more than "turn out" for an election; one might hope that they would also make an intelligent decision.

CONCLUSION

Elections are the vital link between a democracy's citizen and its government. State and local elections afford a citizen the chance to decide matters that are closest to home. In a sense, all elections are state elections because elections for the presidency, Congress, governorship, state legislature, state judiciary, and local offices are conducted by the states. The chief elections officer in California is the secretary of state, and elections occur in the state of California several times every year. There are two main types of elections for offices in California: *primary elections* and *general elections.* The winner of a primary election runs against another finalist in a general election. The winner of a general election attains office. Initiatives, referenda, and recall attempts can be placed on either a primary or a general election ballot.

NOTES

1. Alexis de Tocqueville, *Democracy in America*, trans., ed., and with an introduction by Harvey C. Mansfield and Delba Winthrop (Chicago: The University of Chicago Press, 2000), 197.

2. John Dinan, "Framing a Peoples' Government: State Constitution-Making in the Progressive Era," *Rutgers Law Journal* 30 (1999): 933–985.

3. Alan Rosenthal, *The Decline of Representative Democracy* (Washington, D.C.: Congressional Quarterly Press, 1997).

4. Brian P. Janiskee, "The United States Presidential Election of 2000: The Prospects for Controversy," *Talking Politics: The Journal of the Politics Association* 12 (Winter 2000): 337–342.

5. One should also include the District of Columbia, which acts as a state for purposes of electing a President. This is the result of the Twenty-Third Amendment to the United States Constitution.

6. *California Democratic Party v Jones* (2000).

7. Steve Scott, "And They're Off!" *California Journal* 31 (February 2000): 6–8.

8. Phillip L. Dubois, *Lawmaking by Initiative* (New York: Agathon, 1998).

9. A. G. Block and Charles M. Price, eds., *California Government and Politics Annual: 1998–1999,* (Sacramento: State Net Publications, 1998), 58; James MacGregor Burns et al., *State and Local Politics,* 8th ed. (Upper Saddle River, N.J.: Prentice-Hall, 1996), 114–116; and *The Book of the States, 2000–2001 Edition* (Lexington, Ky.: The Council of State Governments, 2000), 233.

10. California Government Code § 11221.

11. "Propositions," *California Journal* 31 (February 2000): 59–71.

12. Stephen M. Nichols, "State Referendum Voting, Ballot Roll-Off, and the Effect of New Electoral Technology," *State and Local Government Review* 30 (Spring 1998): 106–113.

13. Bessette, *Mild Voice of Reason.*

14. Office of the Secretary of State, *Statement of the Vote, November 3, 1998* (Sacramento, 1998).

15. Using the current CPI index numbers, where 1982–1984 = 100, the gubernatorial election in 2000 was 3.21 times more expensive than the 1976 election in *real* terms. The CPI figures used are those supplied by the Federal Reserve Bank. The CPI index for 1976 is 56.9 and for 1998 is 163.0.

16. See *Buckley v Valeo* (1976) and *Nixon v Shrink Missouri Government PAC* (2000).

17. John M. Carey, Richard G. Niemi, and Lynda W. Powell, "Incumbency and

the Probability of Relection in State Legislative Elections," *Journal of Politics* 62 (August 2000): 671–700.

18. Peverill Squire, "Uncontested Seats in State Legislative Elections," *Legislative Studies Quarterly* 25 (February 2000): 131–146.

19. Putnam, *Bowling Alone.*

Chapter Six

The Legislature

> When . . . public power is in the hands of the people, the sovereign seeks
> everywhere for what is better because it feels bad itself. The spirit of
> improvement then spreads to a thousand diverse objects; it descends to
> infinite details, and above all it is applied to the kinds of improvement
> that can only be obtained by paying.[1]

Progressivism's influence is especially pronounced in the character of
California's legislature, one of America's leading examples of a "professional legislature."[2] A legislature is considered "professional" if its members have high salaries, are supported by a large staff, and convene in
lengthy regular sessions.[3] One of eleven full-time legislatures, California's senate and assembly spend more days in session than all but Michigan and Ohio, which are out of session only on national holidays.
California's senate and assembly members earn annual salaries of
$75,600 and daily working allowances of $110, plus other expenses and
use of a car in Sacramento, making their annual compensation well over
$100,000. This does not include other expenses, including a $240,000
annual budget for office and staff.[4] As generous as this is, such a package
may be far less than a legislator could make in the private sector. What
does this professional legislature do?

LEGISLATION AS PRACTICAL WISDOM

The Nature of Political Decisions

The term "legislature" is derived from the Latin *legis lator,* which means
a "proposer of law." Laws are decisions about the public good and how
best to pursue it.[5] Laws are enforced by the government's coercive
authority, the legitimate power to take life. For example, nothing could
be more mundane than a driver's license; almost every eligible Califor-

nian has this small piece of plastic that allows us the privilege of driving to the movies, the grocery store, or school. These are all ordinary things, but being caught operating an automobile without one would prove to be anything but ordinary. At the very least, one would receive a ticket, which would be noted on one's driving record. With the ticket, the government would levy a substantial fine, and if the fine were not paid, the person fined would be subject to arrest and imprisonment. Inmates are incarcerated under the watch of armed guards—persons authorized to possess lethal force, which is the power to take life. Therefore, even an ordinary driver's license is a reminder of the ultimate power of the government.

Legislation in a Republic

Besides its final and most extreme character, legislation in a republic has another dimension: the ability of constituents to judge the actions of their representatives. The final determination of whether or not elected officials have deliberated in society's best interest rests with the voters.[6] In order for voters to make informed judgments on the merits of their elected officers, they must be able to comprehend adequately the legislation upon which the representative decided. A voter must be able to identify specific issues before the legislature and assess their representative's position.[7] This idea is the core of the American polity.[8]

However, in California the deliberative process is short-circuited to some extent. California's initiative process takes many of the more controversial—not to mention interesting—issues out of the hands of legislators and places them directly before the voters. On the one hand, this initiative process can be seen as a detriment to legislators, for direct democracy diminishes the stature of the legislature as a representative body. On the other hand, direct democracy protects legislators because they can more easily avoid taking a stand on a controversial matter that might come back to haunt them at the next election.

THE BICAMERAL SYSTEM

The California legislature is bicameral, like the United States Congress and forty-nine of the fifty state legislatures.[9] This means that the legislature is divided into two decision-making bodies: a forty-member senate and an eighty-member assembly. Bicameralism serves a vital function in a republic, and Tocqueville described it as a "necessity of the first order."[10] Modern political science scholarship confirms the ancient understanding that bicameralism reduces the potential instability of republican governments.[11] People have little respect for an institution that makes frantic and illogical decisions, which are more possible under unicameral governments.[12] Under bicameralism it is more difficult for a single group to control the entire process, which ensures a more stable policy system that is more likely to produce a reverence for the rule of law; a necessary condition for political life.[13]

DISTRICTING

The method of representation in the California Assembly has always been on the basis of population, with eighty assembly districts of equal population. From 1926 until the 1960s, representation in the senate was based on geography. The state was divided into forty districts that contained whole counties or groups of counties, regardless of population. In *Baker v. Carr* (1962), *Reynolds v. Sims* (1964), and *Wesberry v. Sanders* (1964), the United States Supreme Court declared that such plans of representation violated the Fourteenth Amendment's requirement for "equal protection under the laws." In the opinion of the Court, the individual votes of those living in a senate district of 15,000 people were more powerful than those living in a senate district of 3,000,000. Through these decisions, the Supreme Court established the principle of "one man, one vote."[14] States must define the representation in both chambers of their legislatures on the basis of population, with each district being as equal as possible.[15] As a result, the California senate is divided into forty districts, each containing approximately 800,000 people, and the California assembly is divided into eighty districts, each containing about 400,000 people.[16] Every ten years, California must redraw its legislative districts to ensure that they are, for the most part, equally populated.

Conflicts over Redistricting

As one might imagine, **redistricting** is a highly controversial procedure. The manner in which a district is drawn could determine whether a Republican or a Democrat is elected from that district. The redrawing of districts for political advantage is known as gerrymandering,[17] which in California has been an ongoing source of controversy for over thirty years. The first installment of this drama occurred after the 1970 census, when the Democrat-controlled legislature produced a redistricting plan that was vetoed by Republican Governor Ronald Reagan. The impasse was eventually resolved by a court-ordered redistricting plan. The second installment of the drama occurred after the 1980 census, when the Democrat-controlled legislature presented Democrat Governor Jerry Brown with a plan that he eventually signed. However, the Republicans fought back with a series of successful ballot initiatives that invalidated the plan. As was the case in the 1970s, the courts intervened to impose a new districting plan. The third installment of the drama mirrored the first: In the 1990s, a Democrat-controlled legislature presented Republican Governor Pete Wilson with a plan that was summarily vetoed. After a series of ballot initiatives and counter-proposals by the legislature, the courts, once again, imposed a districting plan. The redistricting plan after the 2000 census was less contentious. This was not because Democrats and Republicans have set aside their differences. Instead, the ease with which the plan was implemented had more to do with tight Democratic control over the legislature and governor's mansion and the GOP's failure to challenge the plan in court.

However, one must not be left with the impression that all of this conflict is petty partisanship. Disputes about redistricting reflect sincere and serious differences of opinion between Republicans and Democrats. The process of redistricting will partially determine which party will form the majority in each legislative chamber, and the majority party has an enormous advantage over the minority party in enacting and passing legislation. Republicans and Democrats have different ideas about the role of government and the policies it should enact.

TERMS

As mentioned earlier, California senators are elected to four-year terms and California assembly members are elected to two-year terms. Furthermore, as a result of a ballot initiative (Proposition 140), members of the senate are limited to two four-year terms and members of the assembly are limited to three two-year terms.[18] As in other states, debate continues over the wisdom of **term limits,** which, in California's case, are among the nation's most restrictive. By increasing the turnover of legislative members, does one increase the power of the governor, other members of the executive branch, career government staff, and interest groups? Is California's government better served? The answers remain to be seen, as term limits are still relatively new.

PARTISAN DIVISION AND ORGANIZATION

Like the United States Congress, the California Legislature is not a continuous body, and no two legislatures are exactly alike. Some members lose elections, retire, or die in office.

At the beginning of each two-year legislature, the members of each chamber organize themselves into a *majority caucus,* which contains those members from the chamber's majority party, and a *minority caucus,* which contains those members from the chamber's minority party.[19]

The Speaker of the Assembly

The presiding officers of the assembly are the **speaker of the assembly,** the majority leader, and the minority leader. The majority and minority leaders are elected by their own party caucuses, and the entire chamber elects the speaker. Like the speaker of the U.S. House, the speaker of the assembly will be a member of the majority party: after a series of straw polls, the majority caucus unites behind one candidate. One historic exception to this rule occurred after the 1994 elections. The Republicans had won a narrow victory over the Democrats and took control of the assembly. However, Republican Assemblyman Paul Horcher defected to the Democratic side, leaving longtime GOP nemesis Willie Brown, a Democrat, as the speaker. Horcher was eventually recalled and the Republicans regained control of the chamber. However, Doris Allen, another Republican defector, switched sides and tilted effective control of the chamber to the Democrats until she too was recalled by her constituents.

The speaker has effective control over who will sit on committees, the assignment of particular bills to committees, who will be recognized on the floor of the chamber, and the amount of financial support members of the majority caucus will receive in their next reelection bid.

President Pro Tempore of the Senate

The titular head of the senate is the lieutenant governor, which mirrors the dual role of the vice president of the United States as president of the senate. Like the vice president, the lieutenant governor rarely becomes involved in legislative affairs. The lieutenant governor's only major legislative responsibility is to cast a deciding vote in the case of a tie.

The effective head of the senate is the **president pro tempore**—most often referred to as the president pro tem. The most influential member of the majority caucus is usually elected president pro tem. He or she chairs the senate **Rules Committee,** which acts as the main governing body of the chamber and supervises such duties as assigning committee seats and monitoring the flow of bills. While not approaching the same relative level of power as the speaker, the president pro tem has become a more pivotal figure in the legislative process in recent years. This is a result of the legacy of David Roberti, the president pro tem of the Democrat-controlled Senate of the 1980s. Senator Roberti's skill and energy set a precedent for subsequent presidents pro tem.

LEGISLATIVE PROCESS

The legislative process, by which bills can become laws, has five stages: introducing a bill, committee consideration, floor consideration, consideration in the other chamber, and consideration by the governor.[20] Only sitting legislators can introduce legislation in the assembly or senate. The governor, lieutenant governor, other government officials not in the legislature, and private citizens cannot introduce legislation into either the assembly or the senate. However, it is common for them to work closely with legislators in the drafting of legislation.

Introducing a Bill

A legislator who thinks a policy proposal would make a good law drafts the idea into a formal document known as a *bill.* Generally speaking, a legislator will propose the broad outline of such a bill and leave it to staff members to fill in the details. Once the bill is drafted, it is then officially introduced into the chamber. The clerk of the chamber assigns it a number according to the order in which it was introduced. If the bill was introduced into the senate, then the letters "SB"—senate bill—would appear before the number, and "AB" appears before the number on assembly bills. It is important to remember that a bill must pass in the same two-year legislature in which it was introduced. If a legislature expires before the bill is enacted into law, the bill must start over again when the next legislature convenes. For example, the legislature that will convene in December 2002 will last until December 2004. If a bill is introduced in August of 2003, it must become a law by December 2004 or it will need to be reintroduced in the next session.

Table 6.1.   Standing Committees

Assembly Committees	Senate Committees
Aging and Long-term Care	Agriculture and Water Resources
Agriculture	Appropriations
Appropriations	Banking
Arts	Budget
Assembly Legislative Ethics	Business
Banking and Finance	Constitutional Amendments
Budget	Education
Business and Professions	Elections
Education	Energy
Elections	Environmental Quality
Energy	Governmental Organization
Environmental Safety	Health and Human Services
Governmental Organization	Housing
Health and Human Services	Insurance
Higher Education	Judiciary
Housing	Labor
Human Services	Legislative Ethics
Insurance	Local Government
Jobs	Natural Resources
Judiciary	Privacy
Labor and Employment	Public Safety
Local Government	Public Employment
Natural Resources	Revenue
Power Outage Preparedness	Rules
Public Employees	Transportation
Public Safety	Veterans Affairs
Revenue	
Rules	
Transportation	
Utilities	
Veterans	
Affairs	
Water	

Sources: California assembly: <www.assembly.ca.gov/govscripts/comdir.idc?> (accessed 6 May 2002), and California Senate: <www.senate.ca.gov/~newsen/committees/standing.htp> (accessed 6 May 2002).

Committee Consideration

The next step after introduction is committee consideration. The Rules Committee in each chamber assigns a bill to a committee according to the bill's subject matter. For example, an assembly farm bill would likely be assigned to that chamber's Agriculture Committee. A senate farm bill would go to the senate's Agriculture and Water Resources Committee.[21]

It is the job of a committee to study the bill and decide whether or not it should be considered by the full chamber.

Committees are the key institutions in each chamber. They hold hearings, conduct studies, and assess the likelihood that a bill will have a reasonable chance of passage on a floor vote. Member and committee staffs analyze the legislation, and lobbyists make their views known. In addition, a nonpartisan legislative analyst, who is appointed by the Joint Legislative Budget Committee, provides members with budgetary, fiscal, and policy information. Committees act as filters through which thousands of bills must pass. Because it is physically impossible for the legislature to vote on every bill introduced in each chamber, most bills are not approved by committees for floor consideration.[22]

Floor Vote and Consideration in the Other Chamber

If a bill survives the committee process, it is brought to the floor for full consideration by the chamber. A majority vote of the entire membership is required for the bill to survive—twenty-one in the senate and forty-one in the assembly.[23] If the bill receives a majority vote, it is sent to the other chamber, where it is reintroduced. If the bill is approved by a majority vote in the other chamber without amending the version sent to it by the original chamber, it is enrolled as an "act of the legislature" and sent to the governor. However, if the other chamber made changes to the bill, the original chamber must agree to these changes or a conference committee will need to be convened. In a conference committee, three members from each chamber meet in order to produce a single, identical bill that could be sent to each chamber. If no compromise can be reached, the bill dies. If a compromise is reached and each chamber approves an identical bill, it is sent to the governor.

Consideration by the Governor

When receiving a bill, the governor has four options: 1) Sign the act within twelve days, which would make it law; 2) do nothing for twelve days and allow the act to become law without a signature; 3) veto the act, which means that the act could only become law if the legislature, voting separately in each chamber, supported it with a two-thirds vote;[24] or 4) invoke what is commonly referred to as a "pocket veto." An opportunity to exercise a pocket veto only happens at the end of a two-year legislature. If the legislature is set to expire and adjourns permanently within the twelve-day consideration period, the governor can simply ignore the act and it will die without any further consideration.

If an act becomes a law, it will go into effect on the following January 1, as long as ninety days have expired since it was approved. Exceptions to this rule are known as *urgency measures,* which, if approved by the governor, go into effect immediately. However, a two-thirds vote is required of each chamber in order to send an urgency measure to the governor.

Other legislation requiring two-thirds approval are budget bills, constitutional amendments, and senate impeachment trials. The two-thirds requirement for a budget bill has a profound effect on California politics because it is rare indeed for a majority party to have two-thirds control of either chamber. Therefore, the minority caucus is intricately involved in the engineering of the state's budget to a degree that is almost unheard of in other states or in the United States Congress.

CONCLUSION

The California Legislature is one of the most professional state legislatures in the United States. Like the United States Congress and forty-nine of the fifty state legislatures, it is bicameral. It is divided into a forty-member senate and an eighty-member assembly. Redistricting plans are proposed every ten years following the census and are often surrounded by partisan controversy. California Senate members are elected to four-year terms and are limited to two terms; California Assembly members are elected to two-year terms and are limited to three terms. The presiding assembly officer is the speaker, and the effective presiding senate officer is the president pro tem.

The legislative process has five stages: introducing a bill, committee consideration, floor consideration, consideration in the other chamber, and consideration by the governor. The governor, lieutenant governor, other government officials not in the legislature, and private citizens cannot introduce legislation into either the assembly or the senate. The Rules Committee assigns a bill to a committee according to the bill's subject matter. If a bill survives the committee process, it is brought to the floor for full consideration by the chamber. If an identical bill is not approved by the other chamber, the bill dies. If the other chamber approves the bill, the governor can sign it, allow it to become law without a signature, veto it, or employ a pocket veto.

NOTES

1. Alexis de Tocqueville, *Democracy in America*, trans., ed., and with an introduction by Harvey C. Mansfield and Delba Winthrop (Chicago: The University of Chicago Press, 2000), 202.

2. James D. King, "Changes in Professionalism in U.S. State Legislatures," *Legislative Studies Quarterly* 25, no. 2 (2000): 327–343.

3. Peverill Squire, "Legislative Professionalism and Membership Diversity in State Legislatures," *Legislative Studies Quarterly* 17, no. 1 (1992): 69–79.

4. Stephen Mansell, *California in Context: A 50 State Comparison of State Legislatures* (Claremont, Calif.: The Rose Institute, 1999), 2, 7, 9, 22.

5. Aristotle, *The Politics*, trans. and introduction by Carnes Lord (Chicago: University of Chicago Press, 1984), 114.

6. Bessette, *Mild Voice of Reason*, 35.

7. For a convincing account of the Founders' belief that voters were capable of such a task, see West, *Vindicating*, 111–130.

8. Edward, J. Erler, *The American Polity* (Washington, D.C.: Crane Russak, 1991), 20–36, 59–67.

9. Nebraska has a unicameral legislature.

10. Tocqueville, *Democracy*, 81.

11. Martin Diamond, *The Founding of the Democratic Republic* (Itasca, Ill.: F. E. Peacock, 1981), 97; and William P. Bottom et al., "The Institutional Effect on Majority Rule Instability: Bicameralism in Spatial Policy Decisions," *American Journal of Political Science* 44, no. 3 (2000): 523–540. See also Thomas H. Hammond and Gary J. Miller, "The Core of the Constitution," *American Political Science Review* 81 (1987): 1155–1174.

12. *The Federalist Papers*, 250.

13. However, in extreme situations, one might be willing to accept extraordinary measures to save a republic.

14. Mark Rush, ed., *Voting Rights and Redistricting in the United States* (Westport, Conn.: Greenwood, 1999).

15. Bernard Grofman, ed., *Race and Redistricting in the 1990s* (New York: Agathon, 1999).

16. One might ask how the Supreme Court could come to this decision in light of the method of representation in the United States Senate. The answer is that the Court recognized the sovereign nature of the states that formed the nation. Geographical subunits of states, such as counties, were never sovereign entities.

17. "Gerrymandering" is derived from the attempt of Massachusetts Governor Elbridge Gerry to rig the 1812 election in favor of his party's legislative candidates. The key to successful gerrymandering is to split up the opposing party's base of support into portions of other districts in which the favored party has majorities.

18. Term limits have side effects: they force candidates to move "up or out," and many term-limited legislators try to move into Congress. See Michael Berkman and James Eisenstein, "State Legislators as Congressional Candidates," *Political Research Quarterly* 52, no. 3 (1999): 481–498; and John R. Hibbing, "Legislative Careers: Why and How We Should Study Them," *Legislative Studies Quarterly* 24,

no. 2 (1999): 149–171. For some of the unanswered promises of term limits, see Dan Walters, "Legislature Risks Return to Elitism," *Fresno Bee* (27 June 2000): A9.

19. For a good examples of election analyses, see, "State Senate," *California Journal* 31, no. 2 (2000): 25–30; and "Assembly," *California Journal* 31, no. 2, (2000): 31–58.

20. For a first-hand account of the process in California, see Michael J. BeVier, *Politics Backstage* (Philadelphia: Temple University Press, 1979).

21. Note that the assembly committee handling farm issues is called the Agriculture Committee and the one in the senate is called the Agriculture and Water Resources Committee. In the Assembly, the Water, Parks, and Wildlife Committee handles water issues. Why the difference? Each chamber is free to divide committee responsibilities as it sees fit. Committees change jurisdictions from time to time, new committees are created, and old ones disbanded.

22. There are three types of committees: standing, select, and joint. Standing committees have regular jurisdictions and remain as entities until the chamber decides to disband them. Select committees are temporary and charged with examining specific, narrowly focused issues. Once the issue is evaluated, the committee is dissolved. A joint committee contains members of both chambers and deals with specific items that affect both chambers simultaneously.

23. This is different from the United States Congress. In that chamber, only a majority *of those voting* is required, as long as a quorum exists.

24. Veto overrides are rare. In effect, a governor's veto nearly always defeats an act. However, if a governor suspects that the legislature would override a veto, the governor might allow an act to become law without a signature. This allows the governor to register disapproval without risking the embarrassment that would come with a legislative override of a veto.

Chapter Seven

The Executive

The executive power of the state has the governor for representative. It is not by chance that I have picked this word, representative. The governor of the state in fact represents the executive power; but he exercises only some of its rights.[1]

The executive branch of the State of California is entrusted with the implementation of laws that have been passed by California or that have been mandated by the federal government. The term "executive" is derived from the Latin word *exsequor,* which means "to carry out." California's executive branch is more fragmented than is the executive branch of the federal government. Whereas the president of the United States is the sole elected head of the federal executive branch, the leadership of California's executive branch is divided among a number of elected officials. This shared responsibility is known as a **plural executive.** Furthermore, the governor's powers over the executive branch are limited by California's civil service system, which has been in place since 1913.[2] A strong civil service system is a key element of the form of administration called a **bureaucracy.** California's executive branch is one of the most bureaucratic in the nation, if not the world, and its level of bureaucratization is a result of the rise of Progressivism since the late nineteenth century.

CALIFORNIA'S GOVERNOR

According to article 5, section 1 of the state constitution, "The supreme executive power of this state is vested in the governor. The governor shall see that the law is faithfully executed." However, the power of the governor to execute these laws is diffused by the plural executive system. The governor does not have a cabinet in the same sense that the president of the United States does. The federal cabinet consists of the heads of the top fourteen executive departments; assuming that the senate approves the cabinet appointees (and such nominations are almost always approved), the president appoints members of the cabinet and has the power to remove them at any time. Therefore, the president has a great deal of control over the policies of the federal executive branch.

The governor of California, on the other hand, cannot remove the heads of the state's most important departments: attorney general, secretary of state, treasurer, controller, superintendent of public instruction, and insurance commissioner. These officials are elected by the voters. However, the governor can appoint people to these directly elected offices, as well as to California's two U.S. Senate seats, when an unexpected vacancy occurs. To make matters even more complicated, the governor cannot always rely on the support of the lieutenant governor, who takes charge if the governor vacates office or is absent from the state. The lieutenant governor is directly elected as well and can often belong to a political party that is different from the governor's. One can only imagine the ramifications this would have on politics at the national level: imagine a scenario whereby former President Clinton would have served with a Republican vice president.

Terms and Elections

According to article 5, section 2 of the state constitution, the governor is limited to two four-year terms.[3] As you read earlier, gubernatorial elections are held in even-numbered, nonpresidential election years, such as 2002, 2006, and 2010. Once in office, a governor can nominate the heads of agencies and departments that do not have directly elected officials. Most of these nominations, however, require legislative approval. The governor also appoints members of the state court of appeals and supreme court, upon confirmation by a judicial commission.

Veto

As described in chapter 6, the governor may exercise a qualified veto over an act of the legislature. The governor may sign a bill into law, veto it and send it back to the legislature, allow it to become law without a signature, or employ a pocket veto. Notwithstanding a pocket veto, all gubernatorial vetoes are subject to legislative override. With a two-thirds vote by each legislature chamber, a bill can become law without a governor's signature. However, such overrides are rare, and vetoes are relatively uncommon. Historically, less than 10 percent of all bills presented to the governor receive a veto. This is not to say that the veto is rarely used because it is ineffective.[4] The threat of a veto can affect legislation as it moves through the senate and assembly. Wise legislators, therefore, would be remiss if they did not anticipate the policy preferences of governors.

Budget

California has what is known as an **executive budget.** State agencies and departments cannot submit budget requests directly to the legislature, but must submit their proposals to the governor. The governor then crafts a unified budget, which is presented to the legislature as a single document. This gives the governor a great deal of leverage over public policy. An even greater form of political leverage is gained by the **line item veto,** with which the governor may veto specific portions of the legislature's annual budget bill without casting a veto against the entire budget. The legislature may still try to override a veto over a particular line item, but since such overrides are rare, the governor can effectively eliminate items from the budget.

Other significant powers of the governor include being the commander in chief of the California National Guard. The National Guard can be called out in an emergency to ensure public order.

In addition to the preceding *formal powers* of the governor, which are shared by governors of most other states, the governor of California has a very important *informal power* that is virtually unique to the Golden State. As the top elected official of the most populous state, California's governor is automatically vaulted to the upper echelon of national politics and is almost always a serious player in presidential elections. Governor Ronald Reagan (1967–1975) was considered a possible contender for the Republican nomination in 1968, nearly defeated incumbent President Gerald Ford for the Republican nomination in 1976, and then went on to receive the nomination in 1980 and was successfully elected twice as the fortieth president of the United States. Governor Jerry Brown (1975–1983) was a serious contender for the Democratic nomination for president in 1976, winning several primaries.[5] For a few months in 1976, there was talk that both the Democratic and Republican nominees in that year's presidential election would have been current or former governors of California.[6] Governor Brown ran again in 1992, and was the last man standing out of the five challengers to the eventual nominee, Arkansas Governor Bill Clinton.

Table 7.1. California Governors

Name	Party	Years in Office
Peter H. Burnett	Independent Democrat	1849–1851
John McDougal	Independent Democrat	1851–1852
John Bigler	Democrat	1852–1856
James Neeley Johnson	American	1856–1858
John B. Weller	Democrat	1858–1860
Milton S. Latham	Lecompton Democrat[a]	1860
John G. Downey	Lecompton Democrat	1860–1862
Leland Stanford	Republican	1862–1863
Frederick F. Low	Union	1863–1867
Henry H. Haight	Democrat	1867–1871
Newton Booth	Republican	1871–1875
Romulado Pacheco	Republican	1875
William Irwin	Democrat	1875–1880
George C. Perkins	Republican	1880–1883
George Stoneman	Democrat	1883–1887
Washington Bartlett	Democrat	1887
Robert W. Waterman	Republican	1887–1891
Henry H. Markham	Republican	1891–1895
James H. Budd	Democrat	1895–1899
Henry T. Gage	Republican	1899–1903
George Pardee	Republican	1903–1907
James N. Gillett	Republican	1907–1911
Hiram W. Johnson	Republican	1911–1915
Hiram W. Johnson	Progressive	1915–1917
William D. Stephens	Republican	1917–1923
Friend W. Richardson	Republican	1923–1927
Clement C. Young	Republican	1927–1931
James Rolph, Jr.	Republican	1931–1934
Frank F. Merriam	Republican	1934–1939
Culbert L. Olson	Democrat	1939–1943
Earl Warren	Republican	1943–1953
Goodwin J. Knight	Republican	1953–1959
Edmund G. Brown, Sr.	Democrat	1959–1967
Ronald W. Reagan	Republican	1967–1975
Edmund G. Brown, Jr.	Democrat	1975–1983
George Deukmejian	Republican	1983–1991
Pete Wilson	Republican	1991–1999
Gray Davis	Democrat	1999–

Source: <www.governor.ca.gov>
[a] A Lecompton Democrat supported a pro-slavery Kansas constitution. The issue split the Democratic Party.

Governors Pete Wilson and Gray Davis have continued in this prominent role. Until withdrawing his candidacy just before the New Hamp-
shire primary in 1996, Governor Pete Wilson (1991–1999) was a
candidate for president. Current governor Gray Davis was a top contender for the vice presidential spot on the 2000 Democratic ticket, a
spot that was eventually filled by Senator Joseph Lieberman of Connecti-
cut. And it would come as no surprise if Governor Davis finds himself
in a similar position, if not as an actual presidential candidate himself
in 2004, assuming that the California budget crisis does not cloud his
prospects.[7]

OTHER ELECTED EXECUTIVES

Lieutenant Governor

The lieutenant governor, along with the other elected executives, is chosen in the same manner as the governor and adheres to the same term
limits and election schedule. The lieutenant governor assumes the office
of governor upon a vacancy in that office or *when the governor is absent
from the state*. This stipulation was cited as one reason why Governor
Pete Wilson, a Republican, decided not to run for president.[8] Governor
Wilson would have been on the campaign trail across the nation in
1996, leaving Democrat Lieutenant Governor Gray Davis as the acting
governor. In addition to the role as the second in command, the lieutenant governor is the president of the California Senate. The activity of the
lieutenant governor in this respect is usually limited to the occasional
tiebreaking vote.

Attorney General

The attorney general of California is the state's top legal officer and is
the chief legal counsel for all state agencies and departments. The attorney general represents the state in all lawsuits, as either a plaintiff or
defendant,[9] and is also the top official in charge of district attorneys and
sheriffs.

Secretary of State

The secretary of state is the chief elections officer in California and is
the official custodian of California's public records. With California's

massive initiative, referendum, and recall system, this is a high-profile position within state government. In fact, with California as a national trendsetter in this area, the decisions of the secretary of state regarding ballot qualifications can garner national attention. This office has attracted recent attention due to the positions and activities of its current officeholder, Republican Bill Jones. Secretary Jones was a proponent of California's recently voided system of blanket primary elections. He also gained national attention by breaking ranks with most other California Republicans to support of Arizona Senator John McCain's bid for the presidency in 2000.[10]

Treasurer, Controller, and Board of Equalization

The treasurer is the state's chief financial officer and has official possession of state tax revenues until they are earmarked by the budget. The treasurer is in charge of all state investments, including selling bonds,[11] and has the official capacity to borrow money on behalf of the state.

The controller disburses state money and acts as the chief auditor for the state.[12] The controller is also on the Board of Equalization, along with four other members, directly elected from California's four equalization districts. The role of the Board of Equalization is to ensure that assessment levels for local property taxes are not set at radically different levels throughout the state.

Insurance Commissioner

The insurance commissioner is charged with oversight of the insurance industry and must approve rate changes. This office was involved in much controversy in 2000, when Commissioner Chuck Quackenbush was forced to resign over a scandal involving his handling of insurance company settlements after the 1994 Northridge earthquake.[13]

Superintendent of Public Instruction

The superintendent of public instruction is unique among California's elected executives because it is the only such office that is elected on a nonpartisan basis.[14] The superintendent is the head of the Department of Education and the chief executive officer of the Board of Education. Therefore, the superintendent is the top official in California's public school system.[15]

Table 7.2. Recent California Elected Executives

Officeholder	Party	Years in Office
Lieutenant Governor		
Frederick F. Houser	Republican	1943–1947
Goodwin J. Knight	Republican	1947–1953
Harold J. Powers	Republican	1953–1959
Glenn M. Anderson	Democrat	1959–1967
Robert H. Finch	Republican	1967–1969
Ed Reinecke	Republican	1969–1974
John L. Harmer	Republican	1974–1975
Mervyn M. Dymally	Democrat	1975–1979
Mike Curb	Republican	1979–1983
Leo T. McCarthy	Democrat	1983–1995
Gray Davis	Democrat	1995–1999
Cruz Bustamante	Democrat	1999–
Attorney General		
Robert W. Kenny	Democrat	1943–1947
Fred N. Howser	Republican	1947–1951
Edmund G. Brown	Democrat	1951–1959
Stanley Mosk	Democrat	1959–1964
Thomas C. Lynch	Democrat	1964–1971
Evelle J. Younger	Republican	1971–1979
George Deukmejian	Republican	1979–1983
John Van De Kamp	Democrat	1983–1991
Daniel E. Lungren	Republican	1991–1999
Bill Lockyer	Democrat	1999–
Secretary of State		
Frank M. Jordan	Republican	1943–1970
H. P. Sullivan	Republican	1970–1971
Edmund G. Brown, Jr.	Democrat	1971–1975
March Fong Eu	Democrat	1975–1993
Tony Miller	Democrat	1993–1995
Bill Jones	Republican	1995–
Treasurer		
Charles G. Johnson	Republican	1923–1956
Ronald A. Button	Republican	1956–1959
Bert A. Betts	Democrat	1959–1967
Ivy Baker Priest	Republican	1967–1975
Jesse M. Unruh	Democrat	1975–1987
Vacant		1987–1988
Thomas Hayes	Republican	1988–1991
Kathleen Brown	Democrat	1991–1995
Matthew Fong	Republican	1995–1998
Phil Angelides	Democrat	1999–

Table 7.2. Recent California Elected Executives (Continued)

Officeholder	Party	Years in Office
Controller		
Harry B. Riley	Republican	1937–1946
Thomas Kuchel	Republican	1946–1953
Robert C. Kirkwood	Republican	1953–1959
Alan Cranston	Democrat	1959–1967
Houston H. Flournoy	Republican	1967–1975
Kenneth Cory	Democrat	1975–1987
Gray Davis	Democrat	1987–1995
Kathleen Connell	Democrat	1995–
Superintendent of Public Instruction		
Roy Simpson	Nonpartisan	1945–1963
Maxwell Rafferty	Nonpartisan	1963–1971
Riles Johnson	Nonpartisan	1971–1983
Bill Honig	Nonpartisan	1983–1992
William Dawson	Nonpartisan	1992–1995
Delaine Eastin	Nonpartisan	1995–
Insurance Commissioner		
John Garamendi	Democrat	1991–1995
Chuck Quackenbush	Republican	1995–2000
Harry Low	Democrat	2000–

Sources: Lieutenant Governor: <www.ltg.ca.gov>; Attorney General: <caag.state.ca.us>; Secretary of State: <www.ss.ca.gov>; Treasurer: <www.treasurer.ca.gov>; Controller: <www.sco.ca.gov>; Superintendent of Public Instruction: <www.cde.ca.gov/executive>; Insurance Commissioner: <www.insurance.ca.gov/docs/index.html>.

OTHER AGENCIES AND DEPARTMENTS

In addition to the departments headed by elected executives, there are a number of agencies and departments headed by appointed officials. Most of these officials are nominated by the governor and confirmed by the legislature. A select group of these agencies and departments are headed by members of the governor's cabinet. However, as stated earlier, the governor's cabinet does not have the same prestige as the president's cabinet does.

BUREAUCRACY

Whether an agency or department is headed by an elected executive or an appointed one, all are organized as **bureaucracies.** Bureaucracies are hierarchical organizations that are organized in three tiers: **operators, managers, and executives.**[16] Operators are the frontline people who "do the job"; in a police department, they would be the patrol officers and detectives, and in a university, they would be the professors. Managers are those who oversee the actions of operators, such as police lieutenants and university deans. Executives are those who are in charge of the overall level of strategic planning, such as police chiefs and university presidents. Bureaucracy is the dominant, almost universal, mode of societal organization in the modern world, and certainly in the state of California.

The social scientist Max Weber recognized the growth of this form of organization nearly a century ago.[17] Prior to that time, most societies were not organized bureaucratically. The predominant mode of organization was what Weber called "charismatic." Charismatic societies are based on personal loyalty, with very little separation between public and private life; in contrast, the intended goal of bureaucracy is to create an administration based on the separation of public and private affairs. The treasury of a nation governed according to a charismatic society would be the personal property of regime's rulers, and the treasury of a bureaucratic regime is strictly separate from the personal fortune of those in charge of the government. The treasury of California is not the personal fortune of the governor, who receives a salary and benefits from the state totaling $175,000 per year. In fact, the governor is not even the highest paid public official in California. This honor belongs to the sheriff of Los Angeles County, who earns $207,000 per year.[18]

The transition from charismatic to bureaucratic administration can be seen most clearly in the changes made in the method of hiring government employees. Prior to the Progressive movement (1880s–1920s), almost all of the government employees were hired on the basis of what was known as *the spoils system,* which held that "to the victor go the spoils of war." The political party that had been victorious in a gubernatorial election, for example, would have had the privilege of filling state government posts with their friends and allies. This system encouraged high level of voter turnout. One can only imagine the turnout today if thousands of jobs depended upon the result of a gubernatorial election. The weakness of this system, however, was its inherent corruption. To solve this dilemma, the leaders of the Progressive movement, of which Governor Hiram Johnson (1911–1917) was a major figure, proposed the creation of a civil service.[19]

The goal of the civil service was to replace a charismatic state government with a bureaucratic one.[20] Hiring decisions in a civil service are supposed to be made on the basis of merit, not on political loyalty. The core principle of the civil service is that government officials should be neutral with respect to politics; they should simply do the job that needs to be done. The strength of this system is that it eliminates much of the corruption in government, but the weakness is that most of those who work in government are now beyond the reach of the voters. During the last change in governors, when Gray Davis took over for the term-limited Pete Wilson, all but a fraction of the government employees remained in office.

CONCLUSION

The executive branch of the State of California is entrusted with the implementation of laws that have been passed by the state or that have been mandated by the federal government. California's executive branch is more fragmented than the executive branch of the federal government is because the leadership of California's executive is divided among a number of elected officers. Furthermore, gubernatorial powers over the executive branch are limited by the strong civil service system of California, which has been in place since 1913. However, the governor's power over the state budget is comparable if not relatively stronger than the president's power over the federal budget. The other elected executives are chosen in the same manner as the governor, adhering to the same term limits. In addition to the departments headed by elected executives, there are a number of agencies and departments headed by appointed officials. A select group of these agencies and departments are headed by members of the governor's cabinet.

NOTES

1. Alexis de Tocqueville, *Democracy in America*, trans., ed., and with an introduction by Harvey C. Mansfield and Delba Winthrop (Chicago: The University of Chicago Press, 2000), 81.

2. Charles Barrilleaux, "Governors, Bureaus, and State Policymaking," *State and Local Government Review* 21, no. 1 (1989): 53–59.

3. This limit was put in place after the passage of Proposition 140.

4. Sarah McCally Morehouse, *The Governor as Party Leader* (Ann Arbor: University of Michigan Press, 1998).

5. "Suddenly Brown's a Winner," *Economist* (22 May 1976): 33.

6. Peter Goldman et al., "How Tight Can it Get?" *Newsweek* (12 July 1976): 16.

7. Steve Scott, "Davis, the Political Powerhouse," *California Journal* 21 (August 2000): 28–31.

8. Jack Germond and Jules Witcover, "Wilson's Pledge Haunted His Candidacy," *The National Journal* 27 (October 1995): 2495.

9. Deanna Bellandi, "California Appeals Sutter-Summit Merger Ruling," *Modern Healthcare* 31 (January 2000): 4.

10. Gil Davis, "Bill Jones: the New Republican Rebel?" *California Journal* 21 (May 2000): 30–33.

11. Julie Tamaki, "Teacher Pension System Dumps Tobacco Stock," *Los Angeles Times* (8 June 2000): A3.

12. Jean O. Pasco, "Controller Sitting on a Pile of Money," *Los Angeles Times* (18 July 2000): B2.

13. Arthur M. Louis, "After Quackenbush," *San Francisco Chronicle* (18 July 2000): C1.

14. This is not to say that officeholders immediately lose their policy preferences upon gaining office. The idea of a nonpartisan office is a residue of the Progressive movement's aim to install public officials who have "neutral competency." The most prevalent manifestation of this idea is with the creation and maintenance of a civil service.

15. Meredith May, "Little Improvement in Dropout Rates from California Schools," *San Francisco Chronicle* (9 June 2000): A3.

16. James Q. Wilson, *Bureaucracy: What Government Agencies Do and Why They Do It* (New York: Basic Books, 1989).

17. Max Weber, "Bureaucracy," in *Max Weber: Essays in Sociology*, ed. H. H. Gerth and C. Wright Mills (New York: Oxford University Press, 1946), 196–244.

18. Tina Duart, "Highly Paid Baca Looks at Raise Reluctantly," *Los Angeles Times* (25 June 1999): B1.

19. Richard Coke Lower, *A Bloc of One: the Political Career of Hiram W. Johnson* (Stanford: Stanford University Press, 1993); and Spencer Olin, Jr., *California's Prodigal Sons: Hiram Johnson and the Progressives* (Berkeley: University of California Press, 1968).

20. Patricia Wallace Ingraham, *The Foundation of Merit: Public Service in American Democracy* (Baltimore: Johns Hopkins University Press, 1995).

Chapter Eight

The California Courts and the Progressivist Legacy

The American judge can only pronounce when there is litigation. He is never occupied except with a particular case; and in order to act he must always wait until he has been seised [presented with a legal dispute]. . . . The American judge therefore resembles perfectly the magistrates of other nations. . . . Nevertheless, he is vested with immense political power. . . . The cause of it is in this sole fact: Americans have recognized in judges the right to found their rulings on the *Constitution* rather than on the *laws*. In other words, they have permitted them not to apply laws that might appear to them unconstitutional.[1]

Just as Tocqueville suggests, we shall consider judges and constitutions together. The progressive features of the California Constitution and polity are sharpened by the state's courts. These courts are rather at odds with founding father Alexander Hamilton's view of the U.S. Supreme Court as "the least dangerous to the political rights of the Constitution." But all the branches of government have been transformed since the Progressive Era; it can no longer be said that courts generally "have neither force nor will but merely judgment."[2] Originally, Progressivism opposed the courts that struck down legislation in the name of property rights. But Progressives such as Supreme Court Justice Oliver Wendell Holmes (a hero to both liberals and conservatives today) were not Hamiltonian justices.[3] Despite the fact that most state court systems, California's included, provide for elected judges and justices, one appreciates nonetheless Hamilton's hope that judges possess qualities of firmness, fortitude, moderation, and integrity as they perform their "duty as faithful guardians of the Constitution."[4]

Hamilton's and Tocqueville's reflections on American judges apply partly to California's situation: Our judges are more political, and the self-restraint and moderation of earlier times have been notably absent from all the branches in California's constitutional development. Tocqueville also thought the U.S. Constitution only changeable by the "will of the people following forms that have been established and in cases that have been foreseen."[5] Under Progressivism, the U.S. Constitution and state constitutions have ceased to be outgrowths of natural rights, and have become as mutable as ordinary legislation—as exemplified by California voters' powers of initiative and referendum. If a constitution can be altered by majority popular vote, then why object to courts that can further alter the constitution and all laws passed under it? And, to extend this logic further, why not elect judges, subject them to recall, and force them to campaign? Thus, California has put a new twist on Tocqueville's famous remark that "[t]here is almost no **political question** in the United States that is not resolved sooner or later into a judicial question."[6]

TYPES OF COURTS

Supreme Court

The California Supreme Court has long been eulogized for its contributions to the development of contemporary law—for example, about product liability laws that enable individuals to sue on account of obvious misuse of an otherwise safe product, such as a cup of hot coffee purchased at a fast-food restaurant. This **supreme court** has been praised and damned for its decisions. The fault lines have not necessarily followed traditional left versus right distinctions. For example, the late Associate Justice Stanley Mosk has been praised by liberals for his role in developing the notion of **"independent state grounds"** and for defending an activist court in the area of criminal law, but he has also won praise from conservatives for his uncompromising assault on racial preferences in *Bakke v. Regents of the University of California,* a position that was substantially toned down by the U.S. Supreme Court. The controversial decisions of the court have included drastic narrowing of the death penalty (now reversed), regulating higher standards of guilt in criminal prosecutions, defending its own use of independent state grounds (which it upheld, against an initiative), and striking down parental notification for a minor daughter's abortion.[7] Especially in the death penalty reversals, the court experienced a shake-up through the recall elections that ended the tenures of Chief Justice Rose Bird and Associate Justices Joseph Grodin and Cruz Reynoso. Their departure enabled then-Governor George Deukmejian to appoint three justices, who, however, did not stay long. The court's previous high reputation among state courts had been shattered, and the effects remain today.

State courts are explicitly bound by Article 6 of the U.S. Constitution to acknowledge the Constitution, and laws and treaties made under it, as "the supreme law of the land." But obviously state courts have their own particular state laws and constitutions to interpret. In California, as in other states, the notion of *independent state grounds* provides for a separate test of state constitutionality that can differ from the federal standard. This notion of a separate constitutionalism, which combines conventional conservative and liberal aspirations, gives the California Supreme Court an unusual significance both within the state and on the national scene. According to former Justice Grodin, "Law students and lawyers are slowly coming to understand that if they have what they regard as a constitutional issue, it is their responsibility to look first to the state constitution."[8]

Yet such contrariness—which some commentators would call independence or creativity—should not be unexpected, given the history of the court.[9] As provided for by the constitution of 1849, the California Supreme Court was to consist of a chief justice and two associate justices elected by the state legislature—or by the people in contested elections—for a term of six years, which was later lengthened to ten years. Early Chief Justice Stephen J. Field, a Democrat, was appointed by Abraham Lincoln to the U.S. Supreme Court in 1863. A veteran of the mines, he would prove to be an intriguing figure who took natural rights seriously as an element of his jurisprudence that emphasized the defense of property rights.[10] Several of his opinions on both the California and U.S. Supreme Courts defended the rights of Chinese immigrants on the basis of the equal protection clause of the Fourteenth Amendment and the federal government's powers in foreign policy. The constitution of 1879 would make the court a chief justice and six associate justices, with twelve-year terms. The legislature could remove judges, including those on the supreme court in certain instances.

Today, the California Supreme Court is still composed of seven justices, who each serve for twelve-year terms. Its formal powers have expanded, and its political character is even more pronounced. The judiciary's formal powers, including those of the supreme court, are described in Article 6 of the state constitution. The court has original jurisdiction in a narrow range of cases, and its major impact is as an appellate court, reviewing the state courts of appeal decisions that are appealed to it. The procedure is similar to that of the U.S. Supreme

Court, which spends much of its time deciding which cases to hear. The California Constitution requires its supreme court to review all death penalty cases; the court may also review the recommendations of the Commission on Judicial Performance, a body of various judges and citizens, and of the State Bar of California concerning the removal and suspension of judges and attorneys for misconduct.

Justices are nominated by the governor after their qualifications are reviewed by the State Bar Association's Judicial Nominees Evaluation Commission. (Consider the George W. Bush Administration's decision to forego this informal step in its judicial nomination process.) Nominees must then be confirmed by the **Commission on Judicial Appointments**. Thus the state legislature is bypassed. The Commission on Judicial Appointments "consists of the Chief Justice, the Attorney General, and the presiding justice of the court of appeal of the affected district . . . or, when a nomination or appointment to the Supreme Court is to be considered, the presiding justice who has presided longest on any court of appeal."[11] If a justice is filling a retiring justice's term, he or she must run for election at the next gubernatorial election for a twelve-year term. The elections have been increasingly divisive, as the numbers of those voting for removal have increased.[12]

Besides the supreme court, which functions mostly as an appellate court, Article 6 establishes three levels of inferior courts. However, the superior courts of all counties other than Kern County have voted to approve the consolidation of the superior and municipal court systems. So for other than Kern County, there are only two courts inferior to the Supreme Court of California—superior and appellate.

Superior and Municipal Courts

There are currently 1,499 superior court judges statewide. The superior and municipal courts function as trial courts. All of their judges must be members of the California bar at least five years prior to their appointment for municipal court judges, and at least ten for superior court judges. Both municipal and superior court judges serve six-year terms. The consolidated **superior courts** and **municipal courts** hear *criminal* cases involving infractions, misdemeanors, and felonies, and the full range of *civil cases*, including divorces. Of the 8.5 million cases filed annually nearly 7.5 million are civil, and the majority of these involve traffic matters.

The district attorney may seek indictment by a grand jury or a pretrial hearing in order to try a felony case. Trials may occur by jury or by judge, as the defendant wishes. The counties that are smaller in population may have only two judges, while Los Angeles County has over 400.[13]

Courts of Appeal

The next highest level is the **court of appeals,** with six districts divided regionally—two in southern California, two in the Bay area, one in Sacramento, and another in Fresno—and a total of ninety-three justices. These courts, which meet in panels of three, handle appeals from all the lower courts and from some public agencies, numbering some 25,000 proceedings. The appeals concern broader issues than those of fact, which are settled at the lower court levels. These issues can involve proper trial procedure, correct interpretation of a law or a constitution (state or federal), or proper application of a law. Given this requirement of expertise, these justices, as they are known, decide which cases to accept and hear them without a jury. Dissatisfied parties may appeal to the California Supreme Court, but the supreme court is not required to hear any appeals other than those for death penalty cases.[14]

FUNCTIONS OF THE COURTS

The dramatic function often played by the U.S. Supreme Court—consider controversial Supreme Court decisions from *McCulloch v. Maryland* to *Bush v. Gore,* from *Dred Scott v. Sanford* to *Roe v. Wade*—overshadows these basic functions of courts. As Abraham Lincoln, who was a country lawyer before entering politics, observed, "Judicial decisions have two uses—first, to absolutely determine the case decided, and secondly, to indicate to the public how other similar cases will be decided when they arise. For the latter use, they are called 'precedents' and 'authorities.' "[15] We will consider both roles.

To exemplify the different functions of the courts and the prosecutors, take the example of the infamous O. J. Simpson murder trial. The District Attorney for Los Angeles County wanted this criminal case tried by jurors downtown rather than from the opulent Bel Air neighborhood where the murders occurred. This strategy, intended to diffuse racial tensions following a conviction of the African American Simpson, produced an overwhelmingly black pool of jurors. The presiding judge of the superior court insisted on a pretrial hearing for an indictment rather than a grand jury, which, he argued, had been swayed by pretrial publicity.

Once the jury declared Simpson innocent, the case could not be appealed because another trial would have meant an unconstitutional double jeopardy. However, he could be (and was) tried civilly in another superior court for damages stemming for his actions, was judged at fault, and paid a considerable fine.

Another example of how the different levels of courts operate is provided by the *Bakke* affirmative action case. Allan Bakke, a Marine veteran of Vietnam and a mechanical engineer, chose to become a doctor despite his established career and age of thirty-two when he first applied for the University of California at Davis Medical School. To make himself competitive for medical school he took undergraduate courses in biology and chemistry. After being turned down twice in 1973 and 1974, Bakke became convinced that the University was admitting applicants far less qualified than he was, solely on the grounds of their race or ethnic origin. The medical school admissions were divided into two different pools: a general applicant pool and a "special admissions" pool of "economically and/or educationally disadvantaged" minorities, from which 16 percent of the entering class would be drawn. None of these were non-Latino whites, and the admission procedures and standards differed dramatically for the two pools. For example, the grade point average for those accepted from the general applicants was 3.5, but that for the special admittees was 2.6. Other dramatic differences were found in standardized test results. In addition, Bakke's test scores placed him well above the average of the general admittee pool.

Bakke's attorney argued before a Yolo County superior court judge that he should be admitted into the medical school and that the UC Davis admissions scheme violated the U.S. Civil Rights Act of 1964 and both the California and U.S. Constitutions. The judge agreed with Bakke on the legal and constitutional issues but denied him admission to the medical school. UC Davis, the judge argued, first had to prove they had not discriminated against Bakke. The university appealed to the California Supreme Court. "At the time, the California Supreme Court was perceived as being the most liberal appellate state court in America,"[16] but the court affirmed the superior court judge, 6–1. Justice Stanley Mosk's opinion ordered the superior court judge to determine if Bakke should be admitted. When the judge would not make that determination, the supreme court ordered Bakke's immediate admission into the medical school.

The U.S. Supreme Court accepted the UC Davis appeal and stayed Bakke's admission, pending its decision on the case. The U.S. Supreme Court split its vote in a complicated 5–4 decision, with two majorities and six opinions, which accepted the U.S. (and implicitly the California) Constitution's Fourteenth Amendment equal protection argument of the California Supreme Court—but not the U.S. Civil Rights Act violation argument. Justice Powell's opinion for the court did not eliminate affirmative action, but only those forms that made race or ethnicity decisive for admitting or rejecting an applicant to a program. Thus, he cut back considerably on California Justice Mosk's sweeping constitutional and legal condemnation of racial and ethnic preferences, but preserved Bakke's right to enter UC Davis Medical School (438 U.S. 265). Subsequently, a California Superior Court later awarded legal fees to Bakke's attorney, payable from the University. In 1982 Bakke, just prior to turning forty-two, graduated from UC Davis medical school. He is currently an M.D. at the Mayo Clinic in Minnesota.

The issue of racial and ethnic preferences remains a controversial one in California. Proposition 209, which invalidated preferences by public employers, passed by a 55–45 margin in 1996. A federal judge who attempted to declare it unconstitutional was overruled by the Ninth Circuit Court of Appeals. Judges played a political role throughout the progress of Proposition 209, such as certifying the ballot description of the proposition, which read:

> The state shall not discriminate against, or grant preferential treatment to any individual or group, on the basis of race, sex, color ethnicity or national origin in the operation of public employment, public education, or public contracting.[17]

The need for California law to yield to the Supremacy Clause of the United States Constitution (article 6, section 2) is vividly illustrated by the U.S. Supreme Court's decision in *United States v. Oakland Cannabis Buyers' Cooperative* (2001). In his Supreme Court opinion, Justice Clarence Thomas declared that federal law does not permit a medical exception to prohibiting the distribution of marijuana. While the decision did not invalidate California's Proposition 215, which permitted the medical use of marijuana, it sets up a clash between state-approved medical marijuana distributors and federal prosecutorial authorities.

The role of the California Supreme Court in checking not just other branches of government but also the initiative process itself is dramatically illustrated by *Raven v. Deukmejian*. In *Raven,* the Court ruled unanimously that Proposition 115, which had restricted the independent state grounds doctrine to make California criminal law consistent with federal constitutional interpretation, was unconstitutional: "The Constitution shall not be construed by the courts to afford greater rights to criminal defendants than those afforded by the Constitution of the United States." The court maintained that the proposition was a revision of the California Constitution, not an amendment, and that only the legislature or a constitutional convention, not an initiative, could revise the constitution. This action of the post–Rose Bird Court, led by Deukmejian appointee Malcolm Lucas and two other Republican appointees, stunned observers and once more confirmed the activist reputation of the court, regardless of its political composition.

In the controversial area of criminal law, California courts may further involve themselves in the constitutionality of "three strikes" legislation, which requires a sentencing judge to impose a penalty of life imprisonment without parole on the third conviction for a crime. Opponents argue that this leads to life terms for stealing a pizza. Proponents point to the increasing numbers of felons leaving California to avoid a "third strike" and life imprisonment. The three strikes law has survived U.S. Supreme Court review, but some argue that the independent state grounds may yet pose a challenge.[18]

Finally, among many other examples, we can note *American Academy of Pediatrics v. Lungren,* which interpreted the right to privacy guaranteed by the California Constitution as a result of an initiative passed in 1972. The court declared unconstitutional the 1987 California statute requiring parental consent for a minor to obtain an abortion. The court opinion, written by Chief Justice Ron George, held that California had independent state grounds, separate from the U.S. Constitution, to declare the law unconstitutional. The explicitly guaranteed right of privacy for Californians, whatever the U.S. Supreme Court held, gave its inhabitants the right of abortion, over any other considerations, parental or otherwise.

CONCLUSION

The California court system, headed by its supreme court, gives the California Constitution much of its meaning. But the dramatic decisions made by the supreme court should not overshadow the work of the civil and criminal trial courts and the courts of appeals, which interpret and apply the law in specific cases. The use of independent state grounds by the California Supreme Court has led to battles over the court's legitimate power; despite an initiative (Proposition 115) restricting its powers in a specific area, the Court declared it unconstitutional. Whether the supreme court can unilaterally shape public policy in controversial areas is highly disputed, as its decisions concerning affirmative action, abortion, and criminal law demonstrate.

NOTES

1. Alexis de Tocqueville, *Democracy in America*, trans., ed., and with an introduction by Harvey C. Mansfield and Delba Winthrop (Chicago: The University of Chicago Press, 2000), 94–95.

2. *The Federalist*, 465.

3. Alan W. Alschuler, *Law Without Values: The Life, Work, and Legacy of Justice Holmes* (Chicago: University of Chicago Press, 2000).

4. *The Federalist*, 470–471.

5. Tocqueville, *Democracy*, 95.

6. Tocqueville, *Democracy*, 256.

7. *Raven v. Deukmejian* (1990). See below for further discussion.

8. Joseph R. Grodin, *In Pursuit of Justice: Reflections of a State Supreme Court Justice*, with a foreword by Justice William J. Brennan, Jr. (Berkeley: University of California Press, 1989), 230.

9. The Supreme Court website offers a summary of its development. See <www.courtinfo.ca.gov/courts/supreme> (21 December 2001).

10. John C. Eastman and Timothy Sandefur, "Stephen Field: Frontier Justice or Justice on the Natural Rights Frontier?" *Nexus: A Journal of Opinion*, 6 (Spring 2001), 121–132.

Field wrote the dissenting opinion in *The Slaughterhouse Cases* 83 U.S. 16 (1873). For Field and his contemporary judges, see also Charles J. McClain, *In Search of Equality*.

11. Article VI, Section 7.

12. See State of California Elections Page: <www.ss.ca.gov/elections/ elections_elections.htm> (accessed 21 December 2001).

13. State of California Court Information Page: <www.courtinfo.ca.gov/reference/documents/supervis.pdf> (accessed 7 May 2002).

14. State of California Court Information Page: <www.courtinfo.ca.gov/reference/documents/ctappbro.pdf> (accessed 7 May 2002).

15. Lincoln, June 26, 1857, in Roy P. Basler, ed., *The Collected Works of Abraham Lincoln* (New Brunswick, N.J.: Rutgers University Press, 1953), vol. II, 400–401.

16. Howard Ball, *The Bakke Case: Race, Education, & Affirmative Action* (Lawrence, Kans.: University Press of Kansas, 2000), 58. We have drawn liberally from Ball's account of the case.

17. For an evenhanded account of this contentious issue by a supporter of affirmative action, see Lydia Chavez, *The Color Bind: California's Battle to End Affirmative Action* (Berkeley: University of California Press, 1998).

18. Brian P. Janiskee and Edward J. Erler, "Crime, Punishment and *Romero*: An Analysis of the Case Against California's Three Strikes Law," *Duquesne Law Review* 39 (Fall 2000): 43–65. The authors also take up the separation of powers issue that may arise if a judge is not given the discretion to impose a sentence of his own fashioning.

Chapter Nine

The Budget and Government Finance

"How is it," I asked, "that you do not put a fee on spirits?" "Our legislators have indeed often thought of it," he replied, "but the undertaking is
difficult. A revolt is feared; and besides, the members who voted such a
law would be very sure of not being reelected."[1]

Budgets are more than mere accounting tools. In the modern administrative state, they have become the chief means by which policies are implemented. The rise of budget politics since the advent of the Progressive
Era poses a serious challenge to the survival of our republican form of
government. Budget rhetoric tends to swirl around complicated jargon
and technical terminology. The ability of a citizen to accurately assess
the actions of their representatives becomes less certain. What is the
meaning of a representative's vote on a massive budget bill, one that
contains thousands of individual expenditure and tax items? Many
expenditure and taxation items are enacted with little fanfare. However,
these same items can have a profound and lasting impact on the ability
of citizens to protect their natural rights to life, liberty, and the pursuit
of happiness.[2]

BUDGET PROCESS

Each year, the governor is required to submit a balanced budget to the
legislature by January 10.[3] The governor sets the overall policy direction
of the proposed budget, as state agencies are required to provide their
budget requests and any other necessary information to the governor.
State agencies and departments cannot send direct budget requests to the
legislature, but must work through a cabinet agency, the **Department of
Finance (DOF)**. The DOF acts as a clearinghouse for the budget requests
of state agencies and departments.[4]

Anticipating economic conditions is crucial in the preparation of a successful budget proposal. Economic downturns can cause a decline in the growth of tax revenues and have the potential to cause budget deficits, which are prohibited by both the California Code and Constitution. An accurate economic forecast will provide the governor and the legislature with a good estimate as to the prudent levels of proposed taxing and spending.

The budget proposal is submitted in the form of a bill, which contains itemized expenditures and the anticipated means of payment for each. The governor's proposal is usually outlined in the annual State of the State Address. This announcement is one of the major policy events in the legislative year. The bill is then officially introduced into each chamber of the legislature by the house and senate budget committees. Before the committees take any further action, the **Legislative Analyst's Office (LAO)** conducts a thorough examination of the budget. The LAO is a nonpartisan organization of policy experts selected by both chambers of the legislature; it assesses the strengths and weaknesses of the governor's proposals. Items that frequently receive close scrutiny by the LAO are the accuracy of the economic forecasts, the level and type of proposed spending, and tax levels. The LAO report is usually completed by the end of February.[5]

At this time, the senate and assembly budget committees begin holding a series of separate hearings. Key participants in these hearings are members of state agencies and departments, as well as lobbyists. The purpose of these hearings is to provide members of the committees with enough information to make the best possible decision. Once the hearings are concluded, each committee produces a proposed budget that is sent to the floor of each chamber for consideration. The two documents are almost never identical. Therefore, at this stage, there are three separate budget proposals: the governor's, the assembly's, and the senate's. The final outcome will be a compromise between the three documents.

The next major step in the process is the governor's May Revision, which includes any adjustments to the original proposal that might have been necessary due to unforeseen circumstances. The budget bill in each chamber must be approved by a two-thirds vote of each chamber—twenty-seven out of forty in the assembly and fifty-four out of eighty in the senate. This requirement is one of the distinguishing features of California government. Since a majority party rarely attains such margins, the two-thirds requirement allows the minority party a vital role in the budget process. In fact, the minority leaders of each chamber are so important to the process that they—along with the governor, speaker of the assembly, and the president pro tempore of the senate—are part of what has come to be known as the Big Five.

Once each chamber produces its version of the budget, a conference committee is convened to reconcile the differences. The conference committee is formed by members from both chambers. Once the conference committee produces a single compromise budget, the document is sent back to each chamber. This compromise budget is sent to the governor upon a two-thirds vote of each legislative chamber. Like the governor's proposed budget, the budget produced by the legislature must be balanced.[6]

After receiving the legislative budget, the governor has the option of reducing or eliminating any spending measure by exercising a line-item veto. Like other vetoes, this is subject to override as well, by a two-thirds vote of each legislative chamber. One might wonder why a governor would bother vetoing an item that has already been approved by a two-thirds vote? Would not a veto override be automatic? This is not necessarily the case. Remember that the compromise budget produced by the legislature is an enormous document. In a spirit of pragmatism, members decide to accept many items of which they do not approve so that other items of which they do approve may become law. However, if the governor happens to exercise a line-item veto over a portion of the budget that a member did not like in the first place, that member and other likeminded members may choose to sustain the governor's veto.

The legislature must complete its work by June 15 in order for the budget to be in place for the start of the new fiscal year, which begins on July 1. However, this deadline is rarely met. It is common for the budget process to move well into August or September. The reason for this is not that the participants fail to live up to their responsibilities. Because the budget has become the principal means by which policy is enacted, differences over the budget reflect the profound and meaningful disagreements that people have over state policy. Therefore, it is not surprising that the process is controversial.

REVENUES AND EXPENDITURES

The process described above refers to the **general fund budget,** the law that authorizes annual spending and taxing. However, there are three other categories of revenues and expenditures that are not taken into consideration in the general fund budget. They are special funds, federal funds, and bond issues. **Special funds** are revenues that are automatically spent on specific areas, such as motor vehicle–related taxes and fees that must be spent on transportation. **Federal funds** consist of grants made by the federal government to the state to carry out particular programs. Special funds and federal funds are, for the most part, beyond the ability of legislature and governor to control. The **bond fund** is not part of the general fund budget due to the unique characteristics of the projects that are in this category. Bond funds, which will be discussed in more detail below, are for long-term capital projects that do not fit into the time frame of an annual general fund budget.

One needs to be cognizant of these different budgets, because of their size. For the 2002–2003 fiscal year, the entire budget—which includes the general fund, special funds, bond funds, and federal funds—was $147.6 billion. Of this, the general fund accounted for only $78.8 billion, special funds for $19.1 billion, bond funds for $2.1 billion, and federal funds for $47.6 billion.[7]

Overall Expenditures

For the 2002–2003 fiscal year, the overwhelming portion of state spending was in the areas of education and welfare. Spending on K-12 education accounted for 31.3 percent of all expenditures, while higher education took up 10.0 percent. Health and human services accounted for 22.4 percent of all state spending. These three areas alone represent 63 cents out of every dollar spent by the state of California. Other significant areas of state spending include business, transportation, housing, and corrections.[8]

Overall Revenues

The money to pay for government expenditures mentioned above comes from a variety of sources. However, the two main methods of collecting state revenue consist of the personal income tax and the sales tax. For the 2002–2003 fiscal year, the income tax provided 53.7 percent of general fund state revenues and sales tax accounted for 28.8 percent. These two areas represent over three-fourths of all state revenues. The next two biggest sources of revenue are corporate taxes and insurance taxes.[9] Local governments, as will be discussed in chapter 10 on local government, also rely on the property tax.

Characteristics of Each Tax

A tax can be either a **progressive tax** or a **regressive tax,** depending upon the relative burden it places on those who pay it. A tax is considered progressive if the rate of taxation increases as income rises. It is considered regressive if this relative rate decreases as income rises, placing a heavier relative burden on those with less income.

Keep in mind that a tax rate is different from the amount of tax collected. For example, assume that the state of California imposed a 100 percent tax rate on all personal income. If one made $50,000 a year, one would pay $50,000 in taxes. What is your best guess as to the amount of revenue the state of California would actually receive? If you guessed $0, you are probably correct. At a 100 percent tax rate, an individual with a full-time job would take home the same amount of money as a person who did not work. Let us assume that the voters became angered over the imposition of such a ridiculous tax and elected new representatives who reduced the rate to 5 percent. What would the state revenues then be? It is hard to estimate, but one could easily imagine that there would be an increased incentive to work. This would allow the state to collect 5 percent of the income. Therefore, at a lower tax rate the state would collect a greater amount of tax dollars.[10] Let us now examine the characteristics of each of the major categories of taxation in California.

Income Tax

The California income tax is progressive, which means that the rate of taxation increases as one is better able to pay the tax and is quite sensitive to the relative financial condition of a taxpayer. The progression of the income tax can be illustrated by the relative tax burdens of people at different income levels.[11] According to recent figures provided by the Legislative Analyst's Office, taxpayers with incomes of over $500,000 a year pay approximately 33 percent of all income taxes, even though they comprise only 0.5 percent of the population. On the other hand, taxpayers with under $20,000 in annual income pay only 1 percent of all income taxes, even though they comprise nearly 40 percent of the population.[12] Furthermore, California's income taxes are indexed to match inflation rates, so that a taxpayer is not pushed into a higher rate bracket simply because wages have kept up with the rise in prices. However, these characteristics make the level of tax revenue collected by the state heavily reliant upon the condition of the economy. During periods of economic growth, the level of income tax revenue increases, but in downturns, the level of revenue falls. Why does the state continue to rely so heavily on the income tax? The answer is that the income tax is a convenient financial instrument for the state because of payroll deduction. It is easy to administer.

Sales Tax

Unlike the income tax, the sales tax is regressive by nature. Everyone, regardless of income, needs to purchase a basic level of food, clothes, and transportation. Those with less money find themselves in the position of paying a larger portion of their income on these necessities. Therefore, taxes on the sales of these items will disproportionately impact those with smaller incomes. However, measures can be taken to mitigate the regressiveness of sales taxes, such as the exemption of food items.

Fees, Item-Specific Taxes, and Property Taxes

In addition to the income and sales taxes, there are a variety of taxes and fees that are peculiar to a particular product. A gasoline tax is perhaps the most regressive tax. One must pay the required rate per gallon regardless of income. The annual automobile registration fee, on the other hand, is indirectly progressive because it is tied to the value of one's automobile. As long as one purchases an automobile that corresponds with his or her income level, then the ability to pay is treated progressively. What about so-called sin taxes on tobacco and alcohol? The effective tax rate could be seen as regressive, but these items are not necessities and a consumer has a great deal of choice over whether or not to use these products and, thereby, pay the tax associated with them. The same would apply to park fees and fishing licenses.

Property taxes, as mentioned previously, are a revenue mainstay of local governments (which are discussed in greater detail in chapter 10). In one sense, the property tax is indirectly linked with income because one pays a larger amount of property taxes on a home worth $500,000 than on one worth $200,000. Assuming that people match the purchase price of a home to their income, it can be said that property taxes are progressive. However, the regressive nature of the property tax comes to the fore due to its unresponsiveness to changes in the homeowner's income. The property tax must be paid regardless of whether or not one is still employed; otherwise, a government may take possession of the home and sell it to collect the required revenue.

Furthermore, one could face an increasing tax burden even when one is prospering in an occupation. If home values suddenly rise at enormous rates, the property tax could become a significant financial burden. A situation like this arose in California during the 1970s. To remedy it, Proposition 13, a measure that limited the increase in property taxes, was approved by voters in 1978. Proposition 13 is just one of a number of influential ballot initiatives in the area of government revenues and expenditures. It is discussed in more detail below and in chapter 10.

BALLOT INITIATIVES

Proposition 13, which was passed in 1978, limits general property tax rates to 1 percent of assessed value and limits the increase in assessed value after a property is purchased or built. Proposition 4, passed in 1979, limits the growth of state spending from year-to-year by either the inflation rate or population growth. Propositions 6 and 7 were approved in 1982 to limit inheritance taxes and require the indexing of income tax rates, respectively.

Passed in 1984, Proposition 37 allowed for the creation of a state lottery, with the stipulation that a certain portion of the funds be earmarked for education. Propositions 62 (1986) and 218 (1996) place strict limits on the ability of local governments to raise taxes. Proposition 98 was passed in 1988 and requires that at least 40 percent of the general fund budget be devoted to K-12 and community college education. Propositions 99 (1988) and 10 (1998) imposed a surtax on cigarettes and other tobacco products, with the stipulation that these funds be earmarked for health programs.

The sales tax on food items, including snacks and bottled water, was repealed after the passage of Proposition 163 in 1992. In the same year, voters decided to increase sales taxes by one-half of a cent, with the requirement that the funds be used to support police and fire departments. Finally, Proposition 39 (2000) rolled back some of the property tax limits put in place by Proposition 13.[13]

BONDS

A **bond** is a certificate that is issued by a government and purchased by individuals or institutions, and major capital projects are supported out of the bond fund. These projects often require several years of construction and entail large initial costs and, therefore, are not well-suited for annual evaluation in the general fund budget process. At a stipulated future date, the government agrees to repay the cost of the certificate, along with a prearranged level of interest. There are three main types of bonds: general obligation bonds, revenue bonds, and special assessment bonds.[14]

General obligation bonds are repaid by a government from its current revenues. In order for these bonds to be issued by the state, each chamber of the legislature must approve them by a two-thirds vote. In addition, they must be approved by a majority of voters. At the local level, most general obligation bonds require majority approval by the legislature of the jurisdiction in question, along with two-thirds support of the voters.

Revenue bonds are repaid by the money generated from the project itself, such as airports and toll roads. Revenue bonds only require a majority vote by the jurisdiction's legislature. *Special assessment bonds* are used by local governments and are paid by assessing property owners according to their relative use of the service provided. These bonds must be approved by a majority of the local legislature, along with votes from owners of a majority of the property that would be affected.

Several firms have established bond rating systems, which are like a person's credit rating, for state and local governments. These systems reflect an entity's history of fulfilling financial obligations. The higher the bond rating, the more confidence a purchaser has that the government will pay the agreed-upon principal and interest by the required date.[15]

CONCLUSION

The governor is required to submit a budget to the legislature by January 10, and this proposal is usually outlined in the annual State of the State Address. The legislature is required to send its version of the budget back to the governor by June 15, but this deadline is rarely met. The largest areas of spending are education and welfare, and the two largest categories of taxation are the income tax and the sales tax. Large capital projects are not funded out of the general fund budget; instead, bonds support these projects. There are three main types of bonds: general obligation bonds, revenue bonds, and special assessment bonds. Several firms have established bond rating systems, which are like credit ratings, for state and local governments.

NOTES

1. Alexis de Tocqueville, *Democracy in America*, trans., ed., and with an introduction by Harvey C. Mansfield and Delba Winthrop (Chicago: The University of Chicago Press, 2000), 215.

2. See John Marini, *The Politics of Budget Control* (Washington, D.C.: Crane Russak, 1991).

3. California Constitution, article 4, section 12.

4. California Department of Finance: <www.dof.ca.gov/fisa/bag/process.htm> (accessed 20 April 2001).

5. Legislative Analyst's Office, *CAL Facts* (Sacramento: Legislative Analyst's Office, 2000).

6. California Government Code, section 13337.5, and California Constitution, article 4, section 12.

7. California Department of Finance, "Chart B, Historical Data, Budget Expenditures, All Funds": <www.dof.ca.gov:8080/html/bud%5Fdocs/backinfo.htm> (accessed 7 May 2002).

8. See California Department of Finance, "Summary Charts": <www.dof.ca.gov/HTML/Budget02–03/00_toc.htm> (accessed 7 May 2002).

9. See California Department of Finance, "Summary Charts": <www.dof.ca.gov/HTML/Budget02–03/00_toc.htm> (accessed 7 May 2002).

10. The logic behind this argument is derived from the Laffer Curve, named after the economist Arthur B. Laffer. See Victor A. Canto, Douglas H. Joines, and Arthur B. Laffer, *Foundations of Supply Side Economics* (New York: Academic Press, 1983).

11. John J. Harrigan, *Politics and Policy in States and Communities,* 5th ed. (New York: Harper Collins, 1994), 70–75.

12. Legislative Analyst's Office, *CAL FACTS:* <www.lao.ca.gov/2000_reports/calfacts/2000_calfacts_pdf_toc.html> (accessed 7 May 2002), 42.

13. Legislative Analyst's Office, *CAL FACTS:* <www.lao.ca.gov/2000_reports/calfacts/2000_calfacts_pdf_toc.html> (accessed 7 May 2002), 26–27.

14. League of Women Voters, *Guide to California Government* (Sacramento: League of Women Voters Education Fund, 1992), 167.

15. These firms are Standard and Poor's, Moody's, and Fitch.

Chapter Ten

Local Government

A very civilized society tolerates only with difficulty the trials of freedom in a township; it is revolted at the sight of its numerous lapses and despairs of success before having attained the final result of experience.

Thus as long as township freedom has not entered into mores, it is easy to destroy it, and it can enter into mores only after having subsisted for a long time in the laws.[1]

Tocqueville believed that he had discovered the essence of democracy in America. The ghost in the American machine was the principle of equality. It was everywhere and nowhere, moving through a myriad of political institutions: "The laws differ and their outward features change, but the same spirit animates them."[2] This spirit had no less a goal than the leveling of all differences, especially those of opinion. This would lead to the development of a centralized administration that would implement a "soft despotism" in the United States.

One of the potential bulwarks against the rising tide of soft despotism was local self-government. From his observations of New England town meetings, Tocqueville argued that a certain degree of local autonomy helped to foster a spirit of civic duty. When considering matters of local government, citizens could more easily notice that their immediate welfare was intimately tied to the welfare of the community. Visceral self-interest could be, in this way, transformed into a **self-interest rightly understood.** If this spirit were to become predominant, America might avoid being dominated by a democratic centralized administration.

If Tocqueville were to examine the condition of local government in California today, he would find that local government in California is a maze of cities, counties, **regional associations,** local agency formation committees, school districts, and other **special districts.** This is hardly what Tocqueville, not to mention the Founding Fathers, had in mind.

CITIES

There are 471 cities in California, and they have primary or shared responsibility for implementing policies in the following areas: police, fire, streets, sewage, storm drainage, sanitation, planning, and zoning. According to state law, there are two basic types of cities: 384 general law cities and eighty-seven charter cities. A **general law city** is governed according to specific provisions in the California Code, and a **charter city** has more flexibility in its management of administrative and fiscal affairs.

The city council is the basic institution of government for California cities. City councils contain at least five members, elected to staggered four-year terms,[3] and their elections can be based on either the ward system or the at-large system. The ward system operates much like elections to the California legislature, with council members being elected from single-member districts (wards) within the city. On the other hand, council members in an at-large system do not represent a specific district within the city. Instead, the entire council is selected in a single citywide election. For example, if a city council were to have five members, the top five candidates in a citywide election would serve on the council, regardless of the neighborhood in which they lived.[4]

Mayors can be directly elected by the city at-large or selected by the council from among its members. A mayoral position can be either weak or strong: Strong mayors have extensive powers to hire and fire city officials, and weak mayors lack these powers but fulfill a ceremonial role. All but the largest cities, which include Los Angeles and San Francisco, employ a city manager as the chief municipal administrative officer. The job of the city manager—sometimes called a city administrator—is to run a city's day-to-day operations and monitor its finances. Since the city manager serves at the pleasure of the city council, his or her level of flexibility is a barometer of the balance of power between a mayor and a city council. Weak-mayor cities are often called council/manager governments and strong-mayor cities are referred to as mayor/council governments.[5]

A sample of the variety of California city governments is displayed in table 10.1. Each city is compared according to 1) whether or not the city has a charter, 2) its method of electing a city council, 3) the strength of the office of mayor, and 4) whether or not there is a city manager. Los Angeles is at one extreme with a mayor/council form of government, while the small Kings County city of Lemoore is the quintessential council/manager city. All of these cities selected have charters except for Lem-

Table 10.1. Comparative Government of Selected California Cities

City	Population	Mayor	Election	Charter	City Manager
Los Angeles	3,695,000	Strong	Ward	Yes	No
San Bernardino	171,000	Weak	Ward	Yes	Yes
Petaluma	54,000	Weak	At-large	Yes	Yes
Lemoore	20,000	Weak	At-large	No	Yes

Sources: Los Angeles mayor: <www.lacity.org/mayor>; Los Angeles city council: <www.lacity.org/council .htm>; Los Angeles demographic information: <www.lacity.org/cao/econ0103.pdf>; City of San Bernardino: <www.ci.san-bernardino.ca.us>; San Bernardino population, *Statistical Abstract of the United States,* table 34: <www.census.gov/prod/2002pubs/01statab/pop.pdf>; City of Petaluma population: <www.dof.ca.gov/HTML/ DEMOGRAP/E5a.xls>; City council of Petaluma: <www.ci.petaluma.ca.us/cclerk/council.html>; City of Lemoore population: <www.dof.ca.gov/HTML/DEMOGRAP/E5a.xls>; City of Lemoore: <www.lemoore.com>; and City Manager of Lemoore: <www.lemoore.com/manager.htm> (all sites accessed 7 May 2002).

oore, the smallest, which is a general law city. The two largest cities in the sample, Los Angeles and San Bernardino, elect city council members by means of a ward system. The two smallest, Petaluma and Lemoore, elect council members through the at-large method. As for the strength of the mayor's office in each city, only Los Angeles has a strong-mayor system. San Bernardino, Petaluma, and Lemoore leave most of the executive decision-making to a council-appointed city manager. As stated above, this sample reflects the general condition of California city government: the smaller the city, the more likely it is to be ruled by a city council, which is elected in an at-large manner.

At-large elections and the employment of city managers are institutions dating from the Progressive Era (1880s–1920s). The goal of progressivism, led in California by Governor Hiram Johnson (1911–1917), was to end the patronage style of governments instituted by large-city political machines. The spoils system was to be replaced with a more rational bureaucratic style of rule.

Questions Faced by California Cities Today

Should the city incorporate adjacent areas? What should be the long-term relationship between the services provided by a city and adjacent unincorporated areas? How can urban sprawl be prevented or successfully managed? These questions are addressed by a **Local Agency Formation Commission (LAFCO)**. There is a LAFCO in each California county, and most consist of representatives from county government, city governments, and the general citizenry.

The most challenging issue faced by LAFCOs is secession, a process whereby a portion of one city seeks to separate itself and form a new city. Currently, the City of Los Angeles is being challenged by several secession movements, most notably in the San Fernando Valley. The Los Angeles County LAFCO determined that the San Fernando Valley can provide the basic level of city services without significant financial damage to rest of Los Angeles,[6] and a secession measure will be placed on the ballot. In order for secession to be approved, the measure must achieve separate majorities in the San Fernando Valley and in the rest of Los Angeles.

COUNTIES

There are fifty-eight counties in California; each county is a legal entity of the State of California and is governed by a five-member board of supervisors. Most of the counties elect their supervisors by means of a single-member district system similar to that of the ward system in city government. The primary areas of policy responsibility for counties are public health, public records, sanitation, sheriff's department, and welfare.

For the most part, county policy responsibilities, including the costs of running the court system, are mandated by the state or federal government. Counties provide approximately 60 percent of the funding for the state's court system. In addition, some counties have contracts with local governments within their jurisdiction to share the costs for certain services. This is called the Lakewood Plan, after the California city that initially adopted this method of providing services. The most common policy areas that fall under the Lakewood Plan are fire and police services.[7]

Most counties in California belong to regional associations. These organizations are quasi-governmental units devoted to cooperation and discussion on issues of regional concern, with mass transit being a prominent example. Counties within a regional association send representatives to serve on a board of directors, share research data, conduct studies, and resolve inter-county disputes. The two largest associations are the Southern California Association of Governments and the Association of Bay Area Governments. The southern California association is formed by representatives from Imperial, Los Angeles, Orange, Riverside, San Bernardino, and Ventura counties. The Bay Area group consists of representatives from Alameda, Contra Costa, Marin, Napa, San Francisco, San Mateo, Santa Clara, and Solano counties.

SPECIAL DISTRICTS

The first special districts in California were created over a hundred years ago to deal with irrigation.[8] In 1900, there were over fifty irrigation districts throughout the state.[9] Since then, the number and variety of special districts has grown considerably. There are 4,079 special district governments in California; included in this are 1,069 school districts, 472 natural resources districts, 369 fire districts, 79 housing and community development districts, and remaining miscellaneous districts that include such things as airports, parks, sanitation, and mosquito control. State legislation allows for the creation of special districts, which are charged with jurisdiction over a specific area of policy and granted carefully enumerated powers. However, while a special district government is limited in its scope, it is still a *government* having the power to tax and enforce regulations.

The most visible special governments in California are school districts. The local government body of a school district is the school board, and the board's chief executive officer is the superintendent. The relationship of the superintendent to the school board is much like that of the city manager to the city council because the superintendent serves at the pleasure of the school board. As is the case in most states, school districts are major political battlegrounds in California, with bilingual education, school prayer, and vouchers among the most controversial issues in state politics. In the 2000 general election, California voters faced two ballot proposals that could have profound and lasting effects on education in the state, Propositions 38 and 39.

Proposition 38 was soundly defeated 71 to 29 percent. Had it been approved, it would have instituted a public school voucher system. At the discretion of parents, the state would have provided $4,000 per student[10] for private or parochial school tuition.[11] Proponents argued, "Control over the education and destiny of California's children must be taken from bureaucrats and given to parents."[12] However, opponents of the measure contended that "not every child will have access to this new system of voucher schools," because "voucher schools will be able to reject students who apply based on their gender, their ability to pay, and their academic and physical abilities."[13] However, proponents of the measure pointed to the successful implementation of a pilot voucher program in Milwaukee, Wisconsin. Milwaukee mayor John Norquist argued that "[a]ll of the things that the critics pointed to as problems haven't happened." Norquist stated further that *public schools* have improved because of the voucher system, due to the fact that the public schools are forced to concentrate on achieving "higher quality" education "that can attract positive attention from parents."[14] The defeat of Proposition 38 could be the death knell for school choice efforts in California.

Proposition 39, which passed by a vote of 53 to 47 percent, offers a departure from the current method of financing local school capital projects. Before Proposition 39, school bond projects required a two-thirds level of support from voters. Furthermore, a similar two-thirds vote was required to exceed the level of taxation allowed under Proposition 13. Under the terms of Proposition 39, the voting requirement for both of these will be decreased from two-thirds to 55 percent. Supporters of the measure all but conceded that it will increase taxes, and stressed additional measures in the proposal that they believed would increase accountability and reduce wasteful bureaucracy. Opponents of the measure argued that Proposition 39 could have the potential to become a significant financial burden to homeowners in that "there is no limit on how much property taxes can eventually increase with passage of 55 percent bonds."[15]

The debate over Proposition 39 can be traced back to what is perhaps the most controversial ballot initiative in California history, Proposition 13 (below). Before the passage of Proposition 13, property taxes were the mainstay of local government finance. Since then, however, local governments have come to rely more heavily on sales taxes, utility taxes, and fees for such things as business licenses, building permits, parks, traffic violations, and trash removal.

PROPOSITION 13

Housing values in California during the early 1970s skyrocketed, causing a dramatic increase in property taxes. The successful passage of Proposition 13 in 1978 led to the rollback of property taxes to 1975 levels, set a rate ceiling at 1 percent of assessed valuation, and limited any potential increase in the tax rate to 2 percent a year. In addition, any new local taxes beyond the property tax restrictions in Proposition 13 can only be passed by two-thirds of the voters in the jurisdiction in question.

The debate over Proposition 13 still rages. Those who oppose the measure argue that before Proposition 13 went into effect, local public services in California were the envy of the nation.[16] After the measure's enactment, opponents argue, California's public services are now among the worst. In addition, and perhaps most disturbingly to the opponents, the fiscal relationships between state and local governments are now so complex that it is beyond the understanding of all but the most elite policy analysts. This, the opponents argue, is a threat to the very nature of democratic government. Lastly, opponents argue that the limit on property tax revenue encourages cities to favor retail development instead of residential development because the cities will be able to harvest more sales tax dollars, which are not under the strict limits of Proposition 13. In the end, this could drive up property costs.

According to the many supporters of Proposition 13, the most fundamental lesson to be learned from this controversy is not the level of taxation alone but also the very nature of the property tax itself.[17] First of all, property tax is one of the most regressive taxes because it is not tied to a person's ability to pay. The homeowner must pay the same amount, or even a higher amount, whether or not the person received a raise, took a pay cut, or lost a job. Second, the property tax is difficult to administer. California counties are in charge of property assessment, and as part of this responsibility, they must provide for an assessment appeals process in the likely event of disputes over assessed value. Lastly, the property tax provides a perverse disincentive to homeowners who decide not to improve their property for fear of an increased assessment.

Those who oppose Proposition 13 and measures like it often fail to grasp the genuine anger that exists about the unjust nature of the property tax.[18] A great deal of effort is spent by the measure's opponents to show how it promotes an irrational system of public finance, as if most citizens look at life through the prism of the public cost accountant.

In addition to Proposition 13, there have been other ballot initiatives affecting local government finance that have gained majority support and been implemented. Among the most significant are Propositions 62 and 218. Proposition 62 was passed in 1986 and mandated that, in addition to an increase in special taxes, any increase in general taxes must be approved by the voters in that jurisdiction. Proposition 218, which was approved in 1996, extended the provisions of Proposition 62 to charter cities.

The opponents of the aforementioned measures decry the loss of local government autonomy in their financial decisions because this loss of control has left local governments more dependent than ever on Sacramento. At first glance, this line of argument does have a potentially conservative cast to it. A repeal of Proposition 13, so the argument goes, would give cities a greater flexibility to deal with problems as they see fit. However, the core debate about Proposition 13 was never about economic *efficiency;* it was about political *justice,* a point that is often lost on many issues beyond that of taxation. In fact, a certain forgetfulness of the centrality of politics is at the core of the debate over what to do about the proliferation of local governments or whether or not it is a problem at all

PUBLIC CHOICE OR
ADMINISTRATIVE RATIONALITY?

The sheer amount and variety of California's local governments is breathtaking. Setting aside any notions of civic participation for the time being, a California citizen would achieve no small feat by simply locating all of the different units of local government that exercise authority in a given area, for "Every citizen in the state is a resident of a dozen or more units of local government."[19] There are 4,608 units[20] of local government in California,[21] and California ranks fourth among all the states in the total number of local government units.[22] To further confuse matters, most of these units do not conform to a common sense geography. It is possible that "two neighbors might be in the same transit district but in different water districts, housing districts, and economic development districts."[23] As opposed to city or county limits that are marked by road signs, the boundaries of special districts are not obvious to passersby. Locating and charting the special districts that have jurisdiction over one's life and property is a daunting task. And even if one did have a professional background in political geography and were able to identify and draw the boundaries for all of the governments in one's area, there is no guarantee that the results of one's labors would provide a clearer picture. It is common for the boundaries of local governments to "have irregular and uneven boundaries and take on a 'Swiss Cheese' design."[24]

The most strident critics of the tangled web of local government are public administration theorists, who argue from the perspective of Progressivist administrative rationality. They state that fragmentation reduces public accountability and causes a lack of coordination that leads to an inefficient administration;[25] therefore, unless the array of local governments is consolidated into a coherent hierarchy, effective and efficient representative government at the local level is impossible.

The most strident supporters of the proliferation of local government units are connected to the public choice (free market) school of economics and have been influenced, in one form or another, by Charles Tiebout.[26] Contrary to the fears of the administrative rationalists, Tiebout argues that citizens would receive more efficient and effective service if there were few (if any) restrictions placed upon the increase of local government units in a state. Local governments would compete with one another for residents and have incentives to achieve a competitive equilibrium between taxes and services. When units of government grow too large, they become disconnected with the citizens who are their customers in the market for public services. The public choice theorists argue that large consolidated governments create a diseconomy of scale that is likely to produce goal displacement within government bureaucracies.[27]

What about the charge by the administrative rationalists that fragmentation makes democratic accountability nearly impossible? Robert Hawkins argued that there is more than one way to evaluate the level of accountability in a government system.[28] In one sense, it is true that voter turnout in special district elections is low and that citizen participation in the decisions of special districts is limited. However, citizen satisfaction in the quality of services performed by local governments is high, and "[c]itizens living in smaller communities consistently had higher levels of satisfaction with local government services than those living in large communities."[29] According to Hawkins, this "pattern held for schools, street maintenance, police protection, zoning, and parks and recreation."[30] Therefore, if we assume that the citizen is best understood as a consumer of government-provided goods, then the best thing to do about the intricate web of California local government services is to increase their number and level of specialization.

CONCLUSION

How might Tocqueville respond to these arguments? In one sense, Tocqueville would probably side with the public choice theorists. He argued that the main contribution to democracy by a strong system of local government is the opportunity to inculcate the citizens with the proper understanding of self-interest. Perhaps the fragmentation of California government is not a bad thing, in and of itself. The breakup of large cities into smaller ones can, perhaps, provide a smaller and more natural environment in which the patriotic transformation of citizens' souls can take place.

In another sense, however, Tocqueville might agree with the administrative rationalists. The patriotic transformation took place in New England towns partly because of the citizens' natural connection to a place with an identifiable character. The properly functioning local government is "so constituted as to excite the warmest of human affections without arousing the ambitious passions of the heart of man."[31] Special districts make a mockery of the natural connections that people have with a specific place, and lie beyond the common-sense experience of almost all citizens. Therefore, the chaotic local government structure in California is a fertile field for the expansion of the administrative state.

NOTES

1. Alexis de Tocqueville, *Democracy in America*, trans., ed., and with an introduction by Harvey C. Mansfield and Delba Winthrop (Chicago: The University of Chicago Press, 2000), 57.

2. Tocqueville, *Democracy*, 531.

3. Councils in larger cities like Los Angeles can have as many as fifteen members.

4. The nature of the relationship between an elected official and their constituents has been broken down by political scholars into two major categories: trustee and delegate. A trustee sees the role of the representative as one who is expected to take into account the views of the constituency but who, in the end, will perform their duty to exercise independent judgment on policy matters. A delegate is a representative who views their role as one who implements the will of their constituents. See Edmund Burke, *Works* (Boston: Little, Brown & Company, 1986; first published 1866), vol. 2, 95–96; Walter Lippmann, *The Public Philosophy* (Boston: Little, Brown and Company, 1955); John C. Wahlke et al., *The Legislative System* (New York: John Wiley and Sons, 1962); Roger H. Davidson, *The Role of the Congressman* (New York: Pegasus, 1969); and Charles G. Bell and Charles M. Price, "Pre-Legislative Sources of Representational Roles," *Midwest Journal of Political Science* 13 (1969): 254–270.

5. Robert L. Linberry and Edmund P. Fowler, "Reformism and Public Policies in American Cities," *American Political Science Review* 61 (1967): 701–716.

6. The technical term used by the LAFCO is whether or not the secession will be "revenue neutral."

7. The Lakewood plan is attractive to cities because it provides them with the means to receive cost-effective services.

8. The United States Census Bureau defines a special district according to the following three criteria: 1) existence of an organized entity, 2) governmental character, and 3) substantial autonomy. See U.S. Bureau of the Census, *1982 Census of Governments* 4, no. 2 (1982), vi.

9. *Guide to California Government* (Sacramento: League of Women Voters of California, 1992), 149.

10. The $4,000 per pupil figure is valid for the first year. In succeeding years, per pupil funding will be the greater of the following three amounts: 1) $4,000, 2) 50 percent of the U.S. mean level of per pupil spending, or 3) 50 percent of the Califor-

nia mean level of per pupil spending. See Secretary of State, *Official Voter Information Guide for the General Election* (Sacramento, 2000), 33.

11. As discussed earlier, there are two types of initiatives: statute initiatives and constitutional initiatives. Propositions 38 and 39 are examples of constitutional initiatives.

12. Secretary of State, *Official Voter Information* (Sacramento, 2000), 36.

13. Secretary of State, *Official Voter Information* (Sacramento, 2000), 37.

14. Secretary of State, *Official Voter Information* (Sacramento, 2000), 37.

15. Secretary of State, *Official Voter Information* (Sacramento, 2000), 41.

16. Jean Ross, "Perspectives on Proposition 13: Flawed Reform," *California Journal* 28 (1997): 26.

17. John J. Harrigan, *Politics and Policy*, 72.

18. Jonathon Coupal, "Perspectives on Proposition 13: Fairness for Taxpayers," *California Journal* 28 (1997): 27.

19. A. G. Block and Charles Price, "Local Government," *California Government and Politics Annual* (Sacramento: StateNet Publications, 1999), 68.

20. San Francisco is a special case, being that it is both a city and a county. For the purposes of this study, I count it in both totals.

21. *Statistical Abstract of the United States* (Washington, D.C., 2000), 309.

22. Only Illinois, Pennsylvania, and Texas have more local government units.

23. Nancy Burns, *The Formation of American Local Governments* (New York: Oxford University Press, 1994), 11.

24. Douglas R. Porter et al., *Special Districts* (Washington, D.C.: Urban Land Institute, 1992), 32.

25. John C. Bollens, *Special District Governments in the United States* (Berkeley: University of California Press, 1957); and Advisory Commission on Intergovernmental Relations, *The Problems of Special Districts in American Government* (Washington, D.C.: ACIR, 1964).

26. Charles Tiebout, "A Pure Theory of Local Government Expenditures," *Journal of Political Economy* 64 (1956): 416–424; and Robert Bisch and Vincent Ostrom, *Understanding Urban Government: Metropolitan Reform Reconsidered* (Washington, D.C.: AEI Press, 1979).

27. For a more thorough analysis of the bureaucratic element of this phenomenon, see Robert K. Merton, "Bureaucratic Structure and Personality," *Social Forces* 18 (1940): 560–68.

28. Robert B. Hawkins, Jr., *Self Government by District: Myth and Reality* (Stanford, Calif.: Hoover Institution Press, 1976).

29. Hawkins, *Self Government*, 52.

30. Hawkins, *Self Government*, 52.

31. Tocqueville, *Democracy*, 67.

Glossary

absentee ballot   A ballot cast before election day and mailed to an appropriate county official.

attention cycle   The level of attention given to a political issue from beginning to end; the public rarely follows an issue with consistent intensity over and extended period of time.

bias   The extent to which a sample fails to accurately measure the opinion of the population.

bond   A certificate issued by a government to fund major capital projects.

bond funds   The pool of money by which capital projects receive financial support.

bureaucracy   A hierarchical organization with the stated of goal of hiring on the basis of merit.

California Constitutions of 1849 and 1879   The pre-statehood constitution of 1849 emphasized the protection of individual rights and limited government; in contrast, the constitutional convention of 1878–1879 produced the California Constitution of 1879, which permitted extensive regulation of economic activity and contained an anti-Chinese article.

centralization   Increased governmental power to include the steadfast gaze of a central authority on the details of everyday political and social life. Tocqueville predicted that the U.S. would develop a growing administrative centralization, and Progressivism brought it to reality.

charter city   A city that has greater autonomy to create its own polices.

Chinese immigration   Chinese who immigrated to work in early California as laborers and who accounted for approximately 8 percent of the population.

Commission on Judicial Appointments   This three-member body consists of the Chief Justice, the Attorney General, and the presiding justice of the court of appeal of the affected district (or, for supreme court nominations, the longest-serving justice on any court of appeal). The governor nominates judges and justices, who then face confirmation by this commission.

Compromise of 1850   Created by the leading statesmen of the time, this set of laws provided for California's entry into the Union as a free state; the possibility of

119

forming slave states out of western territories; the abolition of the slave trade in Washington, D.C.; and the passage of federal fugitive slave laws that provided for the return of escaped slaves to their masters.

court of appeals   Panels of justices that handle appeals from the lower courts in six regions of California. Appeals concern broader issues than those of fact, which are settled at the lower court levels, and can involve proper trial procedure, correct interpretation of a law or a constitution (state or federal), or proper application of a law.

cross-filing   When candidates attempt to gain the nomination of political parties to which they do not belong.

DOF   Department of Finance; the executive agency in charge of preparing the budget.

elite public   The most knowledgeable segment of the population on a given issue.

executive budget   A unified financial request of all agencies and departments, which is presented by the governor to the legislature as a single document.

federal funds   Program grants received from the federal government.

general election   An election in which the winner becomes the holder of the office in question.

general fund budget   A component of the state budget in which most items normally associated with the state, such as education and welfare, are placed.

general law city   A city that is governed according to specific provisions in the California Code.

incumbent   An officeholder who seeks reelection.

independent state grounds doctrine   A doctrine, advanced by various legal scholars and judges, that a state constitution can provide for rights that a person may not have in a U.S. federal court. In California, the doctrine has been applied in the case of criminal defendants, abortion, and the power of initiatives to control the power of the courts.

Johnson, Hiram   A leading Progressive politician of California and national figure who was governor and then senator from 1910–1945. He promoted an array of Progressive measures, including the initiative and referendum, which would drive partisan politics out of the political process.

Judicial Performance Commission   A commission that comprises judges and nonattorney citizens and that monitors judicial conduct.

LAFCO   A local agency formation commission comprised of county government officials who make decisions on such issues as urban sprawl and secession.

LAO   Legislative Analyst's Office; the nonpartisan legislative agency that provides fiscal analysis.

line item veto   The governor's ability to veto specific items in a budget bill without rejecting the entire piece of legislation.

mass public   Those who do not have detailed knowledge of a particular political issue.

muckraking   A style of journalism that is devoted to exposing corruption in business and government.

municipal court   The lowest level of courts, which try minor criminal cases and civil cases. In all but one county, they have been combined with superior courts.

natural rights The inherent rights that all human beings are born with, regardless of time and geography. By limiting the power of government through the requirement that all legitimate power be based on consent, the natural rights doctrines of thinkers such as John Locke (1632–1704) provided the basis for American constitutional government and the first California Constitution.

new media Talk radio, cable television, and the Internet.

nonpartisan election An election for local offices, judicial positions, and for the Superintendent of Public Instruction.

operators, managers, and executives The three-tiered organizational scheme of a bureaucracy.

partisan election An election for legislative and statewide offices.

plural executive An executive branch headed by more than one elected official.

plurality The most votes in an election; could be less than a majority in a race of more than two candidates.

political question A deeply partisan political issue generally to be decided by the elected branches of government, not the courts, such as the question of who should be elected president.

president pro tempore The most powerful member of the forty-seat California Senate.

primary election An election that determines who will be the final contestants in the general election.

progressive tax A tax rate that increases as income rises.

Progressivism A broad-ranging reform movement intended to drive corrupt practices and party bosses out of politics and develop a powerful state led by enlightened administrators. Under Progressivism, strengthened party government would replace the separation of powers, thus transforming American national government into something resembling the parliamentary system.

proportional representation (PR) A method of allocating seats in a legislature on the basis of the total percent received in a national election.

redistricting Redrawing legislative districts to reflect population shifts.

regional association A quasi-governmental association of counties.

regressive tax A tax rate that decreases as income rises.

Rules Committee A key committee in each chamber that assigns bills to a particular committee, thus affecting their chances of passage.

sample A portion of a population used for polling.

self-interest rightly understood The understanding that it is in one's self interest to guard the public liberty.

single member district (SMD) system A method of allocating seats in a legislature on the basis of a series of elections in specific districts.

speaker of the assembly The presiding officer in the eighty-seat assembly.

special district A unit of government created for a narrow purpose.

special funds Money earmarked for specific state programs.

stratified random distribution A method of constructing a sample that recreates the demographic conditions found in the population.

superior court Courts that try criminal and civil cases, including divorces.

supreme court The California Supreme Court consists of seven justices, who serve for 12-year terms. It has original jurisdiction in a narrow range of cases, but its major impact is as an appellate court, reviewing the state courts of appeal decisions that are appealed to it.

term limits   Restrictions on the total number of years a person may serve in a particular political office, such as the assembly, senate, or governorship.

third party   Any party that is not one of the two major parties.

tyranny of the majority   When the majority makes individuals unwilling to think a politically significant thought beyond the beliefs of their peers. The supposed deference of individuals to the majority's presumed wisdom is actually their willingness to flatter majority views in order to be accepted.

Warren, Earl   A nationally renowned Progressive political leader who served as California's attorney general, then as governor for three terms. In 1954 he was appointed Chief Justice of the U.S. Supreme Court, a position he held until 1969.

yellow journalism   A style of journalism devoted to supernatural stories, conspiracy theories, and gossip.

Bibliography

Advisory Commission on Intergovernmental Relations. *The Problems of Special Districts in American Government.* Washington, D.C.: ACIR, 1964.

Ainsworth, Bill. "Astroturf Lobbying." *California Government and Politics Annual: 1998–1999.* Sacramento: StateNet, 1998, 39–40.

Alschuler, Alan W. *Law Without Values: The Life, Work, and Legacy of Justice Holmes.* Chicago: University of Chicago Press, 2000.

Ambrose, Stephen E. *Nothing Like It in the World: The Men Who Built the Transcontinental Railroad 1863–1869.* New York: Simon & Schuster, 2000.

American Academy of Pediatrics v. Lungen (1997) 16 Cal. 4th 307.

Anderson, Terry L. and P. J. Hill. "The Evolution of Property Rights: A Study of the American West," *The Journal of Law and Economics* 28, no. 1 (April 1975): 163–179.

———. "An American Experiment in Anarcho-Capitalism: the *Not* So Wild, Wild West." *The Journal of Libertarian Studies* 3, no. 1 (Spring 1979): 9–28

Aristotle, *The Politics.* Translated with introduction, notes, and glossary by Carnes Lord. Chicago: University of Chicago Press, 1984.

Aristotle. *The Politics.* Translated with introduction and notes by Peter L. Phillips Simpson. Chapel Hill: University of North Carolina, 1997.

"Assembly." *California Journal* 31, no. 2 (2000): 31–58.

Bakke v. Regents of the University of California (1976) 18 Cal. 3d 34.

Baldassare, Mark. *California in the New Millennium.* Berkeley: University of California Press, 2000.

Ball, Howard. *The Bakke Case: Race, Education, & Affirmative Action.* Lawrence: University Press of Kansas, 2000.

Barrilleaux, Charles. "Governors, Bureaus, and State Policymaking." *State and Local Government Review* 21, no. 1 (1989): 53–59

Beard, Charles. *An Economic Interpretation of the Constitution of the United States.* New York: Macmillan, 1913.

Bell, Charles G. and Charles M. Price. "Pre-Legislative Sources of Representational Roles." *Midwest Journal of Political Science* 13 (1969): 254–270.

Bellah, Robert et al. *Habits of the Heart.* Berkeley: University of California, 1985.

Bellandi, Deanna. "California Appeals Sutter-Summit Merger Ruling." *Modern Healthcare* 31 (January 2000): 4.

Berkman, Michael, and James Eisenstein. "State Legislators as Congressional Candidates." *Political Research Quarterly* 52, no. 3 (1999): 481–498.

Bernstein, Sharon, and Robert A. Rosenblatt. "Average HMO Medicare Rate Set to Double." *Los Angeles Times* (16 September 2000): 1.

Bessette, Joseph M. *The Mild Voice of Reason*. Chicago: University of Chicago Press, 1994.

BeVier, Michael J. *Politics Backstage*. Philadelphia: Temple University Press, 1979.

Bisch, Robert, and Vincent Ostrom. *Understanding Urban Government: Metropolitan Reform Reconsidered*. Washington, D.C.: AEI Press, 1979.

Block, A.G. and Charles M. Price, eds. *California Government and Politics Annual: 1998–1999*. Sacramento: StateNet Publications, 1998.

———. "Local Government." In *California Government and Politics Annual*, edited by A. G. Block and Charles M. Price. Sacramento: StateNet Publications, 1999, 68.

Bollens, John C. *Special District Governments in the United States*. Berkeley: University of California Press, 1957.

Bottom, William P., Cheryl L. Eavey, Gary J. Miller, and Jennifer Nicoll Victor. "The Institutional Effect on Majority Rule Instability: Bicameralism in Spatial Policy Decisions." *American Journal of Political Science* 44, no. 3 (2000): 523–540.

Brinkerhoff, Noel. "The Strangest of Bedfellows." *California Journal* 31 (May 2000): 24–28.

Bryce, James. *The American Commonwealth*, vol. 2. Indianapolis: Liberty Fund Press, 1995.

Buckley v. Valeo (1976) 425 U.S. 946.

Burns, Nancy. *The Formation of American Local Governments*. New York: Oxford University Press, 1994.

Burke, Edmund. *Works*. Boston: Little, Brown & Company, 1986.

Burns, James MacGregor, J. W. Peltason, Thomas E. Cronin, and David B. Magleby. *State and Local Politics*, 8th ed. Upper Saddle River, N.J.: Prentice-Hall, 1996, 114–116.

Bush v. Gore (2000) 531 U.S. 98.

Cain, Bruce E., and Roger G. Noll, eds. *Constitutional Reform in California*. Berkeley: University of California, Institute of Governmental Studies Press, 1995.

California Constitution Revision Commission. *Final Report and Recommendations to the Governor and the Legislature*. Sacramento: State of California, 1996.

California Department of Finance, "Chart B, Historical Data, Budget Expenditures, All Funds": <www.dof.ca.gov:8080/html/bud%5Fdocs/backinfo.htm> (accessed 7 May 2002).

California Department of Finance, "Summary Charts": <www.dof.ca.gov/HTML/Budget02-03/00_toc.htm> (accessed 7 May 2002).

California, State of: <www.my.ca.gov/state/portal/myca_homepage.jsp> (accessed 26 December 2001).

California, State of: <www.ss.ca.gov/prd/lobreport00_8qtr/chart1.htm> (accessed 4 May 2002).

California, State of: <www.ss.ca.gov/prd/lobreport00_8qtr/chart4.htm> (accessed 4 May 2002).

California, State of, Court Information Page: <www.courtinfo.ca.gov/reference/documents/ctappbro.pdf> (accessed 7 May 2002).

California, State of, Court Information Page: <www.courtinfo.ca.gov/reference/documents/supervis.pdf> (accessed 7 May 2002).

California, State of, Elections Page: <www.ss.ca.gov/elections/elections_elections.htm> (accessed 21 December 2001).

California Supreme Court: <www.courtinfo.ca.gov/courts/supreme> (accessed 21 December 2001).

California Democratic Party v. Jones (2000) 530 U.S. 567.

Carey, John M., Richard G. Niemi, and Lynda W. Powell. "Incumbency and the Probability of Reelection in State Legislative Elections." *Journal of Politics* 62 (August 2000): 671–700.

Census Bureau of the, United States. *Census of Governments*. Washington, D.C.: United States Government Printing Office, 1982.

Chavez, Lydia. *The Color Bind: California's Battle to End Affirmative Action*. Berkeley: University of California Press, 1998.

Codevilla, Angelo. *The Character of Nations: How Politics Makes and Breaks Prosperity, Family, and Civility*. New York: HarperCollins, Basic Books, 1997.

Commager, Henry Steele, ed. *Documents of American History*. Englewood Cliffs, N.J.: Prentice-Hall, 1973.

Connerly, Ward. *Creating Equal: My Fight Against Race Preferences*. San Francisco: Encounter Books, 2000.

Council of State Governments. *The Book of the States, 2000–2001*. Lexington, Ky.: The Council of State Governments, 2000.

Coupal, Jonathon. "Perspectives on Proposition 13: Fairness for Taxpayers." *California Journal* 28 (1997): 27.

Craft, Cynthia H. "The Economic Silver Lining to Gun Laws." *California Journal* 31 (March 2000): 18–22.

Croly, Herbert. *The Promise of American Life*. New York: Capricorn, 1964.

Davidson, Roger H. *The Role of the Congressman*. New York: Pegasus, 1969.

Davis, Gil. "Bill Jones: the New Republican Rebel?" *California Journal* 21 (May 2000): 30–33.

Dewey, John. *The Public and Its Problems*. Chicago: Swallow Press, 1927.

Diamond, Martin. *The Founding of the Democratic Republic*. Itasca, Ill.: F. E. Peacock, 1981.

DiClerico, Robert. *Political Parties, Campaigns and Elections*. Upper Saddle River, N.J.: Prentice-Hall, 2000.

Douglass, John Aubrey. *The California Idea and American Higher Education*. Stanford: Stanford University Press, 2000.

Dinan, John. "Framing a Peoples' Government: State Constitution-Making in the Progressive Era." *Rutgers Law Journal* 30 (1999): 933–985.

Downs, Anthony. "Up and Down with Ecology: The 'Issue Attention Cycle.'" *The Public Interest* 28 (1972): 38–50.

Dred Scott v. Sanford (1857) 60 U.S. 393.

Duart, Tina. "Highly Paid Baca Looks at Raise Reluctantly." *Los Angeles Times* (25 June 1999): B1.

Dubois, Phillip L. *Lawmaking by Initiative*. New York: Agathon, 1998.

Eck, Diana L. *A New Religious America: How a "Christian Country" Has Become the World's Most Religiously Diverse Nation.* San Francisco: Harper San Francisco, 2001.

Eisenach, Eldon. *The Lost Promise of Progressivism.* Lawrence: The University Press of Kansas, 1994.

Erler, Edward, J. *The American Polity: Essays on the Theory and Practice of Constitutional Government.* Washington, D.C.: Crane Russak, 1991.

———. "Californians and Their Constitution: Progressivism, Direct Democracy, and the Administrative State." *Nexus: A Journal of Opinion* 6 (Spring 2001): 237–256.

Fehrenbacher, Don E. *The Dred Scott Case: Its Significance in American Law & Politics.* New York: Oxford University Press, 1975.

———. *Slavery, Law, and Politics: The Dred Scott Case in Historical Perspective.* New York: Oxford University Press, 1981.

Fehrenbacher, Don, and Norman Tutorow. *California: An Illustrated History.* New York: D. Van Nostrand Co., 1968.

Fenno, Richard F., Jr. *Homestyle.* Boston: Little, Brown, 1978.

Fiorina, Morris. *Divided Government.* 2nd ed. New York: Allyn and Bacon, 1996.

Fuchs, Lawrence H. *The American Kaleidoscope: Race, Ethnicity, and the Civic Culture.* Hanover: University Press of New England, 1990.

Fukuyama, Francis. *The Great Disruption: Human Nature and the Reconstitution of Social Order.* New York: Touchstone Books, 1999.

Galderisi, Peter F., ed. *Divided Government: Change, Uncertainty, and the Constitutional Order.* Lanham, Md.: Rowman & Littlefield, 1996.

Geer, John G., ed. *Politicians and Party Politics.* Baltimore: Johns Hopkins University Press, 2000.

Germond, Jack, and Jules Witcover. "Wilson's Pledge Haunted His Candidacy." *The National Journal* 27 (October 1995): 2495.

Getlin, Josh. "Regarding the Media; for Whom the Polls Toll—the Candidate Who's Trailing." *Los Angeles Times* (18 September 2000): E1.

Glazer, Nathan. *We Are All Multiculturalists Now.* Cambridge, Mass.: Harvard University Press, 1997.

Goldman, Peter Thomas, M. DeFrank, Hal Bruno, and Gerald C. Lubenow. "How Tight Can It Get?" *Newsweek* (12 July 1976): 16.

Grodin, Joseph R. *In Pursuit of Justice: Reflections of a State Supreme Court Justice.* Foreword by Justice William J. Brennan, Jr. Berkeley: University of California Press, 1989.

Grofman, Bernard, ed. *Race and Redistricting in the 1990s.* New York: Agathon, 1999.

Hamilton, Alexander, James Madison, and John Jay. *The Federalist Papers.* Edited by Clinton Rossiter with introduction and notes by Charles R. Kesler. New York: Penguin, Mentor Books, 1999.

Hammond, Thomas H., and Gary J. Miller. "The Core of the Constitution." *American Political Science Review* 81 (1987): 1155–1174.

Hanson, Victor Davis. *The Land Was Everything.* New York: The Free Press, 2000.

Harrigan, John J. *Politics and Policy in States and Communities.* 5th ed. New York: Harper Collins, 1994.

Hawkins, Robert B. Jr. *Self Government by District: Myth and Reality.* Stanford, Calif.: Hoover Institution Press, 1976.

Hayward, Steven. *The Age of Reagan, 1964–1980: The Fall of the Old Liberal Order.* New York: Prima Publishing, 2001.

Hibbing, John R. "Legislative Careers: Why and How We Should Study Them." *Legislative Studies Quarterly* 24, no. 2 (1999): 149–171.

Hubler, Shawn. "Truth and Consequences for the LAPD." *Los Angeles Times* (18 September 2000): B1.

Huntington, Samuel. "The Special Case of Mexican Immigration: Why Mexico Is a Problem." *The American Enterprise* (December 2000): 22.

Ingraham, Patricia Wallace. *The Foundation of Merit: Public Service in American Democracy.* Baltimore: Johns Hopkins University Press, 1995.

Jaffa, Harry V. "The Nature and Origin of the American Party System." In *Equality and Liberty.* New York, Oxford University Press, 1965, 3–41.

———. *Crisis of the House Divided: An Interpretation of the Issues in the Lincoln-Douglas Debates.* Chicago: University of Chicago Press, 1982.

———. *American Conservatism and the American Founding.* Durham, N.C.: Carolina Academic Press, 1984.

———. *A New Birth of Freedom: Abraham Lincoln and the Coming of the Civil War.* Lanham, Md.: Rowman & Littlefield, 2000.

Janiskee, Brian P. "The United States Presidential Election of 2000: The Prospects for Controversy." *Talking Politics: The Journal of the Politics Association* 12 (Winter 2000): 337–342.

Janiskee, Brian P., and Edward J. Erler. "Crime, Punishment and *Romero:* An Analysis of the Case Against California's Three Strikes Law." *Duquesne Law Review* 39 (Fall 2000): 43–65.

Jefferson, Thomas. "First Inaugural Address." March 4, 1801. In *Jefferson.* Edited by Merrill Peterson. New York: Library of America, 1984.

King, James D. "Changes in Professionalism in U.S. State Legislatures." *Legislative Studies Quarterly* 25, no. 2 (2000): 327–343.

Kingdon, John W. *Congressmen's Voting Decisions.* 3rd ed. Ann Arbor: University of Michigan Press, 1989.

Laffer, Arthur B., Victor A. Canto, and Douglas H. Joines. *Foundations of Supply Side Economics.* New York: Academic Press, 1983.

League of Women Voters. *Guide to California Government.* Sacramento: League of Women Voters Education Fund, 1992.

Legislative Analyst's Office, California Legislature. *CAL Facts.* Sacramento: Legislative Analyst's Office, 2000. Retrived online from: <www.lao.ca.gov/2000_reports/calfacts/2000_calfacts_pdf_toc.html> (accessed 7 May 2002).

Les, Kathleen. "Business's Big Guns." *California Government and Politics Annual 1998–1999.* Sacramento: StateNet, 1999: 43–44.

———. "Making the Grade at Hertzberg U." *California Journal* 31 (2000): 32–39

———. "Labor Toils Mightily for a Select Few." *California Journal* 31 (2000): 46–49.

Linberry, Robert L. and Edmund P. Fowler, "Reformism and Public Policies in American Cities." *American Political Science Review* 61 (1967): 701–716.

Lincoln, Abraham. June 26, 1857. In *The Collected Works of Abraham,* vol. 2. Edited by Roy P. Basler. New Brunswick, N.J.: Rutgers University Press, 1953, 400–401.

———. "Address Before the Wisconsin State Agricultural Society, Milwaukee, Wisconsin." September 30, 1859. In *Collected Works,* vol. 3. New Brunswick, N.J.: Rutgers University Press, 1953.

Lippmann, Walter. *The Public Philosophy.* Boston: Little, Brown and Company, 1955.

Lloyd, Gordon. "Nature and Convention in the Creation of the 1849 California Constitution." *Nexus: A Journal of Opinion* 6 (Spring 2001): 23–48.

Louis, Arthur M. "After Quackenbush." *San Francisco Chronicle* (18 July 2000): C1.

Lower, Richard Coke. *A Bloc of One: the Political Career of Hiram W. Johnson.* Stanford: Stanford University Press, 1993.

Mansell, Stephen. *California in Context: A 50 State Comparison of State Legislatures.* Claremont, Calif.: The Rose Institute, 1999.

Marini, John. *The Politics of Budget Control: Congress, the Presidency, and the Growth of the Administrative State.* Washington, D.C.: Crane Russak, 1991.

May, Meredith. "Little Improvement in Dropout Rates from California Schools." *San Francisco Chronicle* (9 June 2000): A3.

Mayhew, David. *Divided We Govern.* New Haven: Yale University Press, 1991.

McClain, Charles J. *In Search of Equality: The Chinese Struggle Against Discrimination in Nineteenth-Century America.* Berkeley: University of California Press, 1994.

McCulloch v. Maryland (1819) 17 U.S. 316.

McWilliams, Carey. *California: The Great Exception.* Foreword by Lewis H. Lapham. Berkeley: University of California, 1999; originally published 1949.

Merton, Robert K. "Bureaucratic Structure and Personality." *Social Forces* 18 (1940): 560–68.

Milkis, Sidney M. *The President and the Parties: The Transformation of the American Party System Since the New Deal.* New York: Oxford University Press, 1993.

Morehouse, Sarah McCally. *The Governor as Party Leader.* Ann Arbor: University of Michigan Press, 1998.

Mowry, George E. *The California Progressives.* Chicago: Quadrangle, 1963.

Netstate: <www.netstate.com/states> (accessed 26 December 2001).

Nichols, Stephen M. "State Referendum Voting, Ballot Roll-Off, and the Effect of New Electoral Technology." *State and Local Government Review* 30 (Spring 1998): 106–113.

Nixon v. Shrink Missouri Government PAC (2000) 528 U.S. 377.

Norris, Frank. *The Octopus: A Story of California.* New York: New American Library, Signet Classics, 1964.

Olin, Spencer, Jr. *California's Prodigal Sons, Hiram Johnson and the Progressives.* Berkeley: University of California Press, 1968.

Olson, Mancur, Jr. *The Logic of Collective Action.* New York: Schocken, 1968.

Ornstein, Norman, Thomas Mann, and Michael Malbin. *Vital Statistics on Congress, 1993–1994.* Washington, D.C.: Congressional Quarterly Press, 1994.

Plunkitt, George Washington. *Plunkitt of Tammany Hall,* as recorded by William L. Riordan. New York: E. P. Dutton, 1963.

Porter, Douglas R., Ben C. In Susan Jakubiak and Richard B. Peiser, *Special Districts.* Washington, D.C.: Urban Land Institute, 1992.

"Propositions" *California Journal* 31 (February 2000): 59–71.

Public Policy Institute of California: <www.ppic.org/facts/likelyvote.mar01.pdf> (accessed 26 December 2001).

Putnam, Robert D. *Bowling Alone: The Collapse and Revival of American Community.* New York: Simon & Schuster, 2000.

Raven v. Deukmejian (1990) 52 Cal. 3d 336.

Regents of the University of California v. Bakke (1978) 438 U.S. 912.

Rodriguez, Richard. *Days of Obligation: Arguments with My Mexican Father.* New York: Viking, 1992.

Roe v. Wade (1973) 410 U.S. 113.

Rohrbough, Malcolm J. *Days of Gold: The California Gold Rush and the American Nation.* Berkeley: University of California Press, 1997.

Rosenthal, Alan. *The Decline of Representative Democracy.* Washington, D.C.: Congressional Quarterly Press, 1997

Ross, Jean. "Perspectives on Proposition 13: Flawed Reform." *California Journal* 28 (1997): 26.

Rush, Mark, ed. *Voting Rights and Redistricting in the United States.* Westport, Conn.: Greenwood, 1999.

Samuelson, Robert J. "Who Cares How Rich Bill Gates Is?" *Washington Post* (2 May 2001): A21.

Schattschneider, E. E. *The Semi-Sovereign People.* New York: Holt, Rinehart, and Winston, 1960.

Schwartz, Stephen. *From West to East: California and the Making of the American Mind.* New York: Free Press, 1998.

Scott, Steve. "And They're Off!" *California Journal* 31 (February 2000): 6–8.

———. "Davis, the Political Powerhouse." *California Journal* 21 (August 2000): 28–31.

Secretary of State, Office of the, California. *Statement of the Vote, November 3, 1998.* Sacramento: State of California, 1998.

Secretary of State, Office of the, California. *Official Voter Information Guide, General Election, Nov. 7, 2000.* Sacramento: State of California, 2000.

Silver, Thomas B. *Coolidge and the Historians.* Durham: Carolina Academic Press, 1982.

Skerry, Peter. *Mexican-Americans: The Ambivalent Minority.* New York: Free Press, 1993.

———. "Mexican Immigration Is Different." In *The American Enterprise* (December 2000), 22.

Slaughterhouse Cases (1873) 83 U.S. 16.

Spalding, Matthew, and Patrick Garrity. *A Sacred Union of Citizens: George Washington's Farewell Address and the American Character.* Introduction by Daniel J. Boorstin. Lanham, Md.: Rowman & Littlefield, 1996.

Squire, Peverill. "Legislative Professionalism and Membership Diversity in State Legislatures." *Legislative Studies Quarterly* 17, no. 1 (1992): 69–79.

———. "Uncontested Seats in State Legislative Elections." *Legislative Studies Quarterly* 25 (February 2000): 131–146.

Starr, Kevin. *Americans and the California Dream, 1850–1915.* New York: Oxford University Press, 1973.

———. *Material Dreams: Southern California Through the 1920s.* New York: Oxford University Press, 1990.

———. *Endangered Dreams: The Great Depression in California.* New York: Oxford University Press, 1996.

"State Senate." *California Journal* 31, no. 2 (2000): 25–30.

Statistical Abstract of the United States. Washington, D.C.: United States Government Printing Office, 2000.

Strauss, Leo and Joseph Cropsey, eds. *History of Political Philosophy.* 3rd ed. Chicago: University of Chicago Press, 1987.

"Suddenly Brown's a Winner." *Economist* (22 May 1976): 33.

Supreme Court, California: <www.courtinfo.ca.gov/courts/supreme> (accessed 21 December 2001).

Supreme Court Elections, California: <www.ss.ca.gov/elections/elections_elections.htm> (accessed 21 December 2001).

Taylor, Michael. "The Reign of S.F.'s Monarch of the Dailies; Hearst Media Empire Started with Examiner." *San Francisco Chronicle* (7 August 1999): A9.

Tamaki, Julie. "Teacher Pension System Dumps Tobacco Stock." *Los Angeles Times* (8 June 2000): A3.

Tarr, G. Alan. *Understanding State Constitutions.* Princeton, N.J.: Princeton University Press, 1998.

Thernstrom, Stephan, ed. *The Harvard Encyclopedia of American Ethnic Groups.* Cambridge, Mass: Harvard University Press, 1980.

Tiebout, Charles. "A Pure Theory of Local Government Expenditures." *Journal of Political Economy* 64 (1956): 416–424.

Tocqueville, Alexis de. *Democracy in America.* Translated, edited, and with an introduction by Harvey C. Mansfield and Delba Winthrop. Chicago: The University of Chicago Press, 2000.

Truman, David B. *The Governmental Process: Political Interests and Public Opinion.* New York: Knopf, 1951.

Turner, Barry, ed. *The Statesman's Yearbook 2001.* London: Macmillan, 2001.

United States v. Oakland Cannabis Buyers' Cooperative (2001) 532 U.S. 483.

Wahlke, John C., Heinz Eulau, William Buchanan, and LeRoy C. Ferguson. *The Legislative System.* New York: John Wiley and Sons, 1962.

Walker, Jack. *Mobilizing Interest Groups in America.* Ann Arbor: University of Michigan Press, 1991.

Walters, Dan. "Legislature Risks Return to Elitism." *Fresno Bee* (27 June 2000): A9.

Warner, Susan. "Drug Firms Get a Dose of Disdain in this Election Year." *San Diego Union-Tribune* (2 September 2000): C1.

Warren, Earl. *The Memoirs of Chief Justice Earl Warren.* Garden City, N.Y.: Doubleday & Co., 1977.

Weber, Max. "Bureaucracy." In *From Max Weber: Essays in Sociology.* Edited by H. H. Gerth and C. Wright Mills. New York: Oxford University Press, 1946, 196–244.

Weissert, Carol S., and William S. Weissert. *Governing Health: The Politics of Health Policy.* Baltimore: Johns Hopkins University Press, 1996.

West, Thomas G. *Vindicating the Founders: Race, Sex, Class, and Justice in the Origins of America*. Lanham, Md.: Rowman & Littlefield, 1997.

White, Louise G. *Political Analysis*. Pacific Grove, Calif.: Brooks/Cole, 1990.

Wilson, E. Dotson, and Brian S. Ebbert. *California's Legislature*. Sacramento: California State Legislature, Office of the Chief Clerk of the Assembly, 1998.

Wilson, James Q. *Bureaucracy: What Government Agencies Do and Whey They Do It*. New York: Basic Books, 1989.

Zigler, L. Harmon, and Hendrik van Dalen. "Interest Groups in the States." In *Politics in the American States,* 2nd ed. Edited by Herbert Jacob and Kenneth N. Vines. Boston: Little, Brown, 1974, 122–160.

Index

abortion, 88, 94–95
administrative state, 18, 116. *See also* bureaucracy
affirmative action. *See* race and ethnicity
agriculture, 2, 46
airports, 104
Alabama, 1, 56
Alameda County, 110
Allen, Doris, 67
America, American. *See* United States
American Academy of Pediatrics v. Lungren, 94
Anderson, Glenn, 81
Angelides, Phil, 81
Aristotle, 4–5
Arkansas, 1
assembly, California. *See* legislature, California
Association of Bay Area Governments, 110
attorney general. *See* executive, California

Baker v. Carr, 65
Bakersfield, California, 1–2
Bakke, Allan, 92
Bakke v. Regents of the University of California, 88, 92–93
Bar, State of California, 90
Barkley, Alban, 20

Bartlett, Washington, 78
Bay area, 91
Bel Air, 91
Betts, Bert, 81
Bigler, John, 78
Bill of Rights, Massachusetts, 6
Bird, Rose, 88, 94
Board of Education, California. *See* executive, California
Board of Equalization, 53, 57, 80
bonds, 80, 99; bond funds, 99–100; bond ratings, 104; general obligation, 104; revenue, 104; special assessment, 104; two-thirds passage requirement, 104
Bono, Sonny, 36
Booth, Newton, 78
borders, x
Boy Scouts of America, xvi
Brown v. Board of Education, 20
Brown, Edmund, Sr. (Pat), 21, 24, 78, 81
Brown, Edmund, Jr. (Jerry), 59, 66, 77–78, 81
Brown, Kathleen, 81
Brown, Willie, 67
Budd, James, 78
budget, 71, 77, 80, 97, 104; allocation in, 100; balance requirement, 99, 104; Big Five, 99; fiscal year, 99; gen-

133

About the Authors

Brian Janiskee received his Ph.D. from Michigan State University and is an assistant professor of political science at California State University, San Bernardino, where he is also a faculty member in the national security studies program. In addition, he is an adjunct fellow at the Claremont Institute and active with the Center for Local Government. He has published several articles in topics ranging from special districts to crime policy to presidential elections.

Ken Masugi received his Ph.D. from the New School for Social Research and is director of the Center for Local Government of the Claremont Institute, with which he has been formally affiliated since 1982. He is editor of *Interpreting Tocqueville's "Democracy in America"* (described in the *American Political Science Review* as representing a "revolution in Tocqueville scholarship") and coeditor of four other books on modern and American political thought.